SIGNALS

How **Questioning** Assumptions Produces **Smarter** Decisions

DAN RIORDAN

Post Hill
PRESS

A POST HILL PRESS BOOK
ISBN: 978-1-68261-455-6
ISBN (eBook): 978-1-68261-456-3

Signals:
How Questioning Assumptions Produces Smarter Decisions
© 2018 by Dan Riordan
All Rights Reserved

Cover art by Allan Ytac

Post Hill Press
New York • Nashville
posthillpress.com

Published in the United States of America

ACKNOWLEDGMENTS

The list of people who have supported me and been with me—through the good and the bad—is a long one. I especially want to say thank you to my parents, who have always encouraged me to pursue independence and education. For all the others, I am forever grateful for your love and support. My mistakes are many, and in my pursuit of selfish illusions, I have hurt many. I ask your forgiveness for my lack of integrity. I am proudest of the fact that I have had the strength to realize I was lost in the game of illusions. I have learned to love myself and hope to help as many people as I can avoid some of the missed Signals and Illusion traps that I fell into. I hope this book can help others scale themselves and their organizations.

TABLE OF CONTENTS

FOREWORD

Generally missed and often ignored, the signals that are emitted by all living forms, and from within the business entity, are a critical facet that, when accurately interpreted and used effectively, can provide advanced indicators for the operative design and continued refinement of our organizations, our communities, and even how we choose to live our lives. In the book, *Signals*, Dan takes the reader on a vibrant and practical journey into uncovering and leveraging these often hidden and overlooked feedback indications that are forever present in your company, on your team and in your life. These are the hints of a future to come absent active involvement.

While at Gonzaga University studying for my dream job in Aeronautical Engineering, I found myself increasingly dissatisfied with the extent to which the body of study failed to take into consideration the human factors relating to how people dynamically interact both with the physical and virtual worlds. My growing unease (the signals I was receiving) eventually led me to make a seemingly dramatic and nonsensical shift, what Dan refers to in this book as a "cauliflower moment," at which time I switched majors to finish my undergraduate studies as a Psychology and Industrial Relations major at the University of Maryland.

From that time, I recall that my three favorite courses, the aggregate of which turned out to represent the exact intersection that continues to inspire me, were: Psycho-physiology and Biofeedback, Computer Programming, and Environmental Psychology. They say that "hindsight is 20/20," and it is now clear that the circuitous network of signals that guided me through college, combining an engineering education with the social sciences, set me up for a dynamic and rewarding career that continues to evolve and deliver indications that guide me into new opportunities every day.

When Dan first introduced me to the thesis for this book, *Signals*, I was instantly attracted to the elegance of the logic and the profound impact that this approach can have on the way that business leaders approach predictive analytics, artificial intelligence, and lead/lag indicators to anticipate, measure, and improve the health of their organizations and teams. Throughout life, there are hidden signals, feedback mechanisms, that, following the theories of thermodynamics and other engineering disciplines, can quickly inform leaders and teams in advance of certain events occurring. This is true in all aspects of how teams and organizations organize and operate, and, it is true within our communities and family structures.

I'm excited to share these insights with you and to enter a conversation together that is certain to challenge and advance the current hypotheses of organization design, the client experience, and employee engagement.

Let's get this conversation started!

Dianna Wilusz
CEO and Founder, The Pendolino Group

PREFACE

What has *your* world become? Many of us have let assumptions guide us to default actions. These default choices have big implications. Whether you work at a large or small company, are an employer or an employee, coach, teacher, or parent, your Beliefs, Values, and Illusions (BVIs) trigger unconscious reactions to signals you are receiving. A signal conveys information and we all need to be receiving these signals and changing our reactions to them. Through the years, I noticed many patterns in myself and others showing that we react from our BVIs and make decisions from our assumptions which can lead to self-deception.

Through seven different start-up companies and broken relationships in both work and personal life, I spent many years believing I knew what was right, but I still experienced negative outcomes. That led me to develop a way to question assumptions that would help me scale my own limits and those of our organization. We all want choices and control but, by not being open to new information from our signals, we slowly lose our freedom and our world becomes more complex and less autonomous.

Signals: Question Assumptions to Make Smarter Decisions in Business and Life

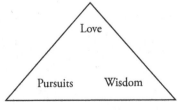

INTRODUCTION

This book is intended for everyone, whether you work at a large or small company, are an employer or employee, a coach, teacher, parent, and so forth. In today's workplace, we are all driving for the workplace of 2020 and beyond. We are expecting big shifts with things like artificial intelligence, connected devices, and other technology solutions. With the integration of these resources, we increasingly are expecting the workforce of 2020 and beyond to be innovative, imaginative, faster, etc. These expectations are driven by inside-out thinking…improve the systems, set goals better, set values….

Signals is about teaching you how to be open to new information using outside-in thinking. Recognizing situations in which you rely on assumptions and self-deceptions to trigger your reactions. We react on the signals coming from all sorts of systems from unconscious instinct. Very few of our reactions are based on reason. In our lives, the systems around love, our pursuits, and acquisition of knowledge are all areas that are fraught with flawed unconscious instincts and bad assumptions. If we ignore the signals, we lose the ability of those signals to drive us to different outcomes because we didn't harness the energy from each signal. The universal energies are constantly speaking to us, but often, we're not listening. Understanding the signals requires effort and the ability to realize that we can't impact our lives and the world around us by self-perfecting. We have to impact from the viewpoint of listening and the principle of progression mindset. The principle of progression is all about realizing as

11

we close our worlds to the signals coming in, we lose the ability to make progress. In the work world, we are saying that millennials are different, but in my work world experience I have asked our millennials what is most important to them…it is to be making progress. In life and in work we are all the same. Being open to the signals and making progress is vital and is driven by outside-in thinking. The outside environmental factors we are all facing are daunting. We are expecting employees to be highly engaged, imaginative, intellectually curious, and to take ownership but that will be increasingly difficult given the environmental factors they are all dealing with. We are seeing an explosion of type 2 diabetes, obesity, metabolic collapse, cardiovascular disease, and cancer…An estimated 7.7 million pounds of antibiotics are prescribed to Americans every year, equaling over 800 prescriptions for every 1,000 individuals. There has been a scary increase in the number of cases of autism from 1 in 5,000 in 1975 to 1 in 42 today. If the current trajectory continues, somewhere between 2030 and 2045—a mere 13 to 28 years from now—autism is projected to affect 1 in 3 children. At that point, it will be impossible to maintain human productivity in any given sector. Today, 1 in 2 adults also struggle with mental health problems. In 1900, that ratio was 1 in 100. All of these disease statistics and more correlate with dramatic changes to the energies that power our bodies. If we want workplaces that thrive, we have to go beyond the inside-out and drive to helping our people and ourselves get past their assumptions.

I have dubbed the moments when we truly listen to the signals and realize that assumptions we have made are wrong, as Cauliflower Moments. This started a few years ago when I was at a crossroads in all aspects of my life. I was 50 years old, failing in my personal life, overweight, suffering from high blood pressure, and dealing with a rapidly expanding company. As I started awakening myself, I realized my systems that were failing were similar to all the failings in the world. Changing my lens from self-perfecting to loving myself and others, I realized that to scale our company, I had to first scale myself, and to scale myself, I had to start listening to signals, asking some serious questions, and getting myself back into a progression–principle mindset. These signals were everywhere and yet I had been operating without accepting any of them. I was so firmly locked in the mindset that I was separate from the universe that I had no reason to question the signals. My pursuit of selfish desires led me to ignore the signals and I was driven only by my reflex reactions.

My awareness of the signals began with workplace topics and proceeded to subjects of health, and subsequently led me to personal epiphanies that I never imagined I would have. Back then, I looked at things from my ego and thought the assumptions with which I was running my life had no practical consequences. As a business person, I ran things by the numbers and the data. Don't get me wrong; the data and the facts are important, but I have come to realize there is something bigger. The systems of our lives all have an order and energy to them. The people in our organizations drive the energy into our lives and businesses. My pathway to new perceptions began by realizing the more we understand that our real role is to help people be happier and drive positive feelings into our businesses and our lives, the more we can optimize our workplaces and the people who work in them.

I was evaluating my decisions in business and life from a place of my beliefs, values, and illusions (hereafter known as BVIs) that I had developed to guide all my decisions; it was all about me. On one hand, our ego gives us as humans the ability to judge good and evil, but on the other side, the BVIs are recursive patterns into self-obsessive behaviors that control our freedom of thought.

As our company was scaling and I was scaling myself, I had a deeper realization. The more our egos drive us to believe our BVIs are right, our selfish desires and selfish BVIs start to confine us and we lose our freedoms just when we believe we are gaining them. Slowly, each decision based on the BVIs leads to less freedom, more complexity, and ultimately chaos to ourselves and those around us. We have lost the principle of progression by which everything is governed.

Signals continually come into our lives and our businesses minute by minute. How we respond to these signals determines how we experience our lives. Typically, our reactions to the BVIs are based on one or more assumptions which leads to a "no" mindset. This mindset means you say "no" to new information, "no" to a new idea, and "no" to a new feeling. This No Mindset = Loss of Freedom. The more we focus on self and desires, the more we lose the signals, and the more freedom is lost.

The key is to get past the BVIs and assumptions and to process these signals from a "yes" mindset. With a "yes" mindset you don't make an emotional BVI-based decision; instead, you react by questioning more deeply and being open to new information. You move from the no mindset where the knowledge of man powers your decisions, to a yes mindset where the knowledge of mankind can power your decisions.

You have "Choiceability" on who and how the BVIs that you follow were created. Do your BVIs come from government? Big business? Friends? Family?

Let me explain this concept differently. When I am buying an apple, I am buying the apple because I assume it is going to fulfill my desire for vitamins, ease my hunger, provide sweetness, or some other need. I don't just pick the apple on the top. The apple on top might have been dropped, probably was touched the most, and may be the oldest one that the store strategically placed there for a quick sale. I dig deeper in the pile and examine each one to see if it meets my criteria, and then I pick the one that I believe fulfills my need. I am basing this choice on digging past the initial layer to get to what I believe is a better apple—or a better outcome.

Even after this process, not until I actually bite into the apple will I determine if it satisfies my needs and wants. Tasting it is the only way to see if my assumptions were right.

We all need to drive past our BVIs and assumptions and bite the apple in every signal. By letting someone else determine your BVIs, you are conducting unplanned experiments on your happiness. Essentially, other people are handing you the apple they want you to have.

While this book is focused on the workplace, I will offer insights on health and personal matters as they relate to the workplace and optimal performance. Our organizations suffer primarily from our BVIs and the poor decisions they drive. Regardless of the industry you work in or the size of your company, most likely your approach to work isn't driving optimal results. In spite of access to the latest technology along with available data, many of us work under "false" assumptions. We're constantly being manipulated and—for the sake of our physical and mental well-being as well as our ability to succeed—it's time to stop. These moments—when you stop and question your assumptions—are Cauliflower Moments.

Assumptions based on false information are becoming an epidemic. From the daily decisions made at corporations to everyday choices on what we eat, assumptions are causing catastrophic issues. In the workplace, worker satisfaction is at an all-time low and the costs of poor productivity have skyrocketed. In 2015, an estimated $550 billion was lost because of poor worker engagement. In terms of our well-being, mental hospitals are filled to capacity, jails are jammed full, more people are in therapy and developing addictions each year, which are all major problems signaling that we are not doing so well in the long term. Forty-five percent of the population—or 140 million people in the U.S. alone—have chronic disease. That number is expected to increase to 170 million in 15 years. Clearly, something isn't right. We weren't created with defects in our instincts; we have been programmed with defective reflex reactions.

Over and over again, I see companies ignore signals from their workforce, their customers, and their suppliers. I am a veteran of seven different start-ups; I am currently COO of ThinkHR, a fast-growing company in Silicon Valley. Many of the issues we help employers solve, start by employers assuming that any dissatisfaction or uncertainty will disappear. However, in many cases, the assumptions around what the teams know or don't know have critical ramifications. For instance, you have probably made assumptions that your teams know how to interview, evaluate performance, manage, and so forth. In fact, these assumptions lead to poor employee retention, lower innovation, unhappy customers, and increasing disorder over time.

Since 1970, technology and science have collided to inflict influence and control over everything we believe. Science has learned to manipulate our basic physiology, and technology has figured ways to get in front of us to manipulate what we think and feel. This combination has driven us to all become trapped into what I call our Box of Limitations. This Box of Limitation is filled with the BVIs that have been programmed into us. To break through this unconscious control, we need to stop for key moments when we truly question our BVIs. These moments allow you to break through to the truth. You must start to ask: Why do you believe that? Why is it so important to you? What has influenced your choices?

This transition, from unconscious thinking to inspired conscious thinking and learning, is an exciting process. The systems in your life are sending signals all the time, but you may not be listening. In the natural world, we have the unique ability to choose to act on a signal or not. This Choiceability can drive us to question our BVIs and have new Cauliflower Moments in our lives.

Signals + Choiceability + Cauliflower Moments = Progress

CHAPTER 1
The Principle of Progression

We all suffer and don't reach our full potentials, not because of a lack of luck, abilities, or something else, but because people want to stay hidden in the façade of their certainties. I was very comfortable in the life I had created with my BVIs. However, those BVIs were blocking my ability to process the signals coming into my world, which in turn was leading me to lose my ability to decode the signals, and therefore my ability to have freedom of thought. I was locked into a service-of-self versus service-to-others mentality and all progress was halted.

> *"It is impossible to begin to learn that which one thinks one already knows."—Epictetus*

Epictetus was a Greek philosopher who believed "individuals are responsible for their own actions, which they can examine and control through rigorous self-discipline." This insightful statement amplifies how firmly we can be stuck in our BVIs.

By staying in the certainties of our BVIs, we are disconnecting ourselves from the natural processes of the world. We are designed to decode signals and develop innovative solutions and we must allow ourselves to start processing the signals again. We have all been lulled into the equation that Comfort + Conformity + Convenience = Certainty. However, this calculation is completely wrong. The certainty we have today is a certainty based on someone else's view, not our own feelings. The most profitable thing we can all learn is to truly know ourselves.

The first stop in the journey of *Signals* and why we are all being fooled by the façade is to dive into some "Brain Basics."

The Brain

This three-pound organ inside your skull drives your intelligence, character, personality, and every decision you make. This is not a new concept. The Greek physician and "father of medicine" Hippocrates wrote about it back around 400 B.C.

> "...and men ought to know that from the brain, and from the brain only, arise our pleasure, joy, laughter and jests, as well as our sorrows, pains, despondency and tears... I am of the opinion that the brain exercises the greatest power in man."

How does our brain form beliefs? What our senses see, hear, feel, and taste must pass through regions of the brain generally understood to govern emotion, reward, and primal feelings. All processes go through some truth-testing process in the brain. The mind generates beliefs, disbeliefs, uncertainties, and certainties by passing these sensations through different areas of evaluation and patterning. Our interpretation of these feelings is governed by our stored memories from experiences in our past that have created assumptions about what is right and wrong, good or bad, or harmful and helpful. These assumptions that we believe are true are not necessarily true in the *worldly* context.

It is your brain that decides whether you should buy that new shirt on an impulse or save your money for another more valuable goal, whether you spend the evening working to get ahead in your job or spend your energy and focus on mastering the latest video game. It decides whether you say yes or no to drugs, alcohol, and smoking or stop eating when you are beginning to feel full, or eat the entire cake because you deserve and "need" it. Your brain is the control center for every decision and action in your life. To be successful you must start with a healthy brain.

The signals coming into your brain can be likened to your car's dashboard. Important messages about the systems in your life—your organization, your health, your relationships, and so on—are all coming into your brain utilizing a vast array of sensors. When something goes wrong, a signal flashes a warning light. In cars, if it is serious, the warning light glows brighter or stays on constantly. At some point all cars will have a warning signal for a vehicle malfunction. We usually pay attention to the signals in our cars. We don't simply "unwire" (disconnect) the warning light. We take the car to the shop and make sure whatever is wrong gets fixed.

However, in life, we seem to ignore the signals. When our body signals us, we either "unwire the lights" by self-medicating or ignore the signals until something critical occurs.

Chronic disease is skyrocketing, largely because people ignore symptoms. Debt is increasing because people don't pay attention to their finances. In business, we blame others, procrastinate, and overlook issues. This leads to higher employee-turnover rates, slowing of product development, increased dissatisfaction in the workforce, and other reactions.

You need to effectively read and efficiently react to the signals coming into your business in order for it to grow and expand. For example, recently an employee of our company behaved erratically one day. This person had been a great employee for more than a year but suddenly behaved strangely one day. I could have ignored the signal and just written it off as that person is having a bad day, but instead, the next day I went to the remote office and asked what was going on. They then unloaded all their frustration about their manager not listening to them. We had a productive talk and a month later, that employee thanked me for changing their viewpoint and helping them realize they were acting in a way that was going to cause them to lose their job. I listened to the signal; instead of processing the behavior from the BVIs and assumptions, I went right to the questioning. I asked myself what had changed. This wasn't random; something was up. I forced myself to question, I talked to the manager and our HR team, and I went straight to the employee.

The key to effecting change is to start processing the signals differently. Stop reacting from the BVI-layer and the assumptions they have generated. You need to change your focus from the obvious to the underlying. Begin questioning the signals coming from your employees, your customers. and your enterprise in general. Signals come in many forms such as product-development delays or retention issues. Start with the questions and don't let any assumptions or BVIs cloud your view.

At the center of our BVIs is a belief that we all have a defect. When the signal comes in that you are sleepy, you feel that your body is failing you. Or you get a bad grade on a test and you feel you are inadequate, etc. Each time, we ignore the signal because we brush it off thinking we have a defect. I want to stress that the defect isn't in you; the defect is in the environment around you as well as the energy state you are in. By listening to signals, you will get past the defect mentality and get to a questioning mentality.

I have been using the **Signals** concept to question the façade of the BVIs and get to the **Cauliflower Moments**. Let me explain:

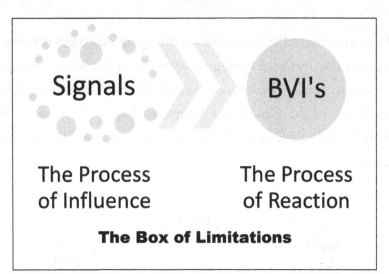

When a signal comes in, for each system in our lives, we have developed a Box of Limitations that guide our decisions. Most of us stay within the reaction of our BVIs because that is how we have done things in the past. More often than not, these are patterns we have seen in ourselves or have been told by the media or "experts in the field" who influence how we interpret these signals and then how we react to them. We learn to feel, react, and think in one way; not until that way is proven to be wrong do we change our viewpoints.

I call these changes to our deeply held beliefs our Cauliflower Moments. As noted in the introduction, a few years ago, I received signals from every system in my life all at once. To scale our company, I had to dramatically change myself. Failed relationships personally and professionally: my health was failing, I went to the doctor to discover my blood pressure was skyrocketing. The signals were coming in from all systems of my life. My BVIs and the "certainties" were leading me to failure. I had to make a choice: was I going to listen and question, or was I going to stay stuck in my BVIs and wave the white flag?

I was completely disconnected from my signals. My Boxes of Limitations were preventing me from having the freedom of intellectual opportunity and new discoveries. The funniest part of this whole awakening has been the evolution of the Cauliflower Moments. I spent 52 years of my life thinking I hated cauliflower. My Box of Limitation around cauliflower was amazing.

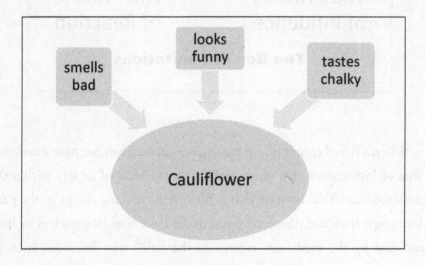

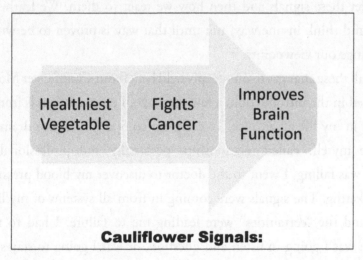

Knowing that I needed to improve my well-being, I thought that perhaps I should start to eat it. Soon after, I was offered cauliflower "mashed potatoes" and remembering the signals about its benefits, I cautiously took a bite. Wow! I loved it! How was it possible that I had hated this vegetable for so long? My BVIs had become my certainties…and they were wrong.

This became my Cauliflower Moment, or my CM as we will call them. It started me down the path of questioning all systems and the Box of Limitation I had formed around them.

Cauliflower has become this amazing metaphor for all systems. On the surface, the vegetable looks so simple. But it is more complex: it provides nutrients that are heavily involved in the signaling process of the brain and body. Cauliflower is an amazing powerhouse of nutrition, it has a structure similar to the brain, and it has a recursive fractal pattern to it that contains similar patterns but gets more and more complex as you magnify it. In a similar way, our decisions driven by BVIs, may look simple on the surface but these simple assumptions are driving more complexity and disorder into your world.

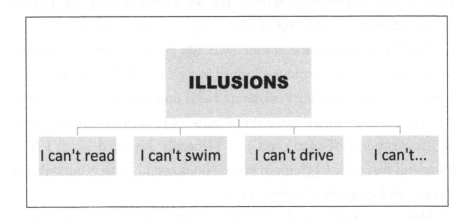

Now I understand a signal will lead me to a series of questions that will let me discover the next Cauliflower Moment of unlocking a new perception. This concept is invigorating. When I get a signal and I have my BVI around what action to take, I have a series of questions that are all based from a biblical passage, 1 Corinthians 8:2 (CEB), "If anyone thinks they know something, they don't yet know as much as they should know."

My questions include:

- Is this something I know…or think I know?
- What more do I need to know or can I know about this?
- What am I supposed to understand in this situation?
- What information would really help me?
- Where did my BVIs come from on this signal?

I'm learning to pay more attention to where the signal is coming from and what my immediate reaction to it is rather than assuming I already know what to do. I question everything from relationships, workplace matters, and even my own health. I test my assumptions against facts so I'm not allowing the opinions of others to dictate my BVIs.

In order for you to discover your own CMs, you first need to understand where your Box of Limitations is formed in each area of your life. In today's world, our basic operating systems are based on a set of stories that form our Boxes of Limitations. You will find many of these limitations disguised as "Conventional Wisdom says" or "Generally Regarded as…." I have found out that these labels mean there is no data and no facts but only the unsupported opinions of some people.

Here are a few examples of marketing messages where the Box of Limitations and the BVIs led people to certainties that weren't true.

- Radium and U. S. Radium Corp were marketed as safe but turned out to be deadly....
- Smoking was good for you at one point...imagine that.....
- Fat was bad for you...now it is good for you.

> You may think a banana is just a banana, but it's not. Dole and other growers have made the creation of a banana into a mini-science. Sales records show that bananas whose peel color is Pantone color 13-0858 (otherwise known as Vibrant Yellow) are less likely to sell than bananas whose peel color is Pantone color 12-0752 (called Buttercup), which is one grade warmer, visually, and seems to imply a riper, fresher fruit. Therefore, these companies plant bananas under conditions most likely to produce the "right" color.

Personal limitations include statements like:

- I can't swim...but then you learn how to swim.
- I can't ride a bike...then you can.
- I can't whistle...then you can.

We have more than 6,000 thoughts in a day and 90 percent of them are the same as yesterday! The certainties around those 90 percent keep us trapped in our Boxes of Limitations.

Key Takeaways

The Principle of Progression: Dare to drive beyond certainties when signals appear.

Get comfortable in the Intellectual Suspense of not knowing.

Realize when you are reacting from your BVIs.

Learn to start asking questions including:

- Is this something I know, or think I know?
- What more can I or should I know about this?
- What am I supposed to understand here?

Look for signals coming from all areas of your enterprise and your life.

CHAPTER 2
The Decision-Making Process

Respect the idea that your perspective will always be evolving.

The Decision-Making Processes we use at work and in our personal lives are identical, and as I discussed in Chapter 1, the brain drives everything.

Processing signals from the Box of Limitations and the BVIs versus making decisions from the outside-in keeps us locked into a world of Illusions versus Reality. As we examine decision making, you'll see there's a great deal of theory and science behind what drives decisions. At the core of the BVIs in the corporate world are the following Overriding Signals that I listen for and then drive into my questions when I hear them:

- Validating decisions: Have you ever been in a meeting or a discussion where somebody recounts a story from a past work experience to validate a decision they want to make? What is happening in that scenario? Is the memory of the past experience genuine or is it a manufactured memory? Psychologists describe this trait as positive re-interpretation. What does this mean? With past experiences, our memories bring the best parts to the surface—and the annoying, tiresome parts fade into the forgotten background. Thus, an illusion is created!

- Evaluating experiential memories much more favorably then material experiences.
- Burden of proof: What are the things you will evaluate in your work and personal decisions? Key drivers include statistics as proof, credentials showing authority, surveys as a scientific method of proof, and case studies of real-life successes. For each of these drivers, as companies we need to make sure we are not selling Illusions, and as consumers, we need to evaluate reality, not the BVIs a company/product wants us to believe.

As individuals and as part of corporations, we get attached to these BVIs. This attachment causes fear, the fear causes sameness, and this sameness causes corporations to lose their competitive edge. When you feel that you already know an outcome, you won't process new information. That's why you should respect the idea that you don't need to know everything. Let your questioning and curiosity drive you.

I recently read an article on the impact of Facebook. The article said, "People are now having to go to psychologists because their Facebook timelines are all an Illusion.They only put the best moments online and when they look back at it, they realize it isn't all as it seems...their actual life is messy...and they want the life they portrayed online!!"[1] We need to shrink the gap of who we are versus who we want to be.

At the root of decision-making, the signals are loud and clear in most companies. Keep in mind a subtle fact: the idea that a person has been changed when they are overpowered is a false assumption. Some common signals in the decision process that can lead to Cauliflower Moments are:

- **Signal:** A common refrain is that technology will drive better decisions. The Cauliflower Moment is that enhancing the availability of information used by people to make their decisions is more critical than upgrading their technologies. Everyone is so enthralled with technology, but it doesn't add more knowledge. Instead, you want to drive more access to information.
- **Signal of Desire:** Is the strong influence of a few people driving the overall decision process? For example, the strong voice of a founder, salesperson, or operating executive drives decisions without letting people commit to the questioning process and deal with the facts.
- **Signal:** Decisions get too inward focused. This occurs because we are focused on protecting what we have versus what the signals are telling us.
- **Signal:** Decisions are a comparison of outcomes with the obvious tendency to focus on outcomes that are enjoyable. Usually, we are too emotionally attached to an outcome causing us to be subjective rather than objective in our observations. It is this category of signal that is often made in businesses.
- **Signal of Delay:** Decision process slows down to a crawl. Leaders are worried about mistakes or second guessing so actions are delayed. Everything is clear with hindsight so instead you should use your questions to reach a place of clarity and knowledge. Knowledge is energy and energy drives innovative thinking.
- **Signal of Defense:** Bad decisions don't get killed. Inertia seems to take over and keep perpetuating

> *"CEOs always act on leading indicators of good news, but only act on lagging indicators of bad news."—Andy Grove*

decisions already made. It is the fear of perceived failure that holds us back from moving forward.

The ability to recognize these signals is vital and the key signals of desire, delay, and defense helped me to establish a new way of evaluating company decisions. I use my quick list of questions to evaluate these signals:

- Is this something they know or think they know? What more do I need to know or can I know about this?
- What am I supposed to understand in this situation?
- What information would really help me/us?
- Where did our BVIs come from on this signal?

To drive good decisions, you need to get your colleagues and your teams to care and be committed to developing new perspectives, rather than relying on their BVIs. To develop these new perspectives, we need to realize we are susceptible to outside influences from a range of sources including advertising, politicians, late night infomercials, science, technology, and more. These influencers don't have our best interests in mind and in fact, are controlling more and more of our personal and professional lives.

Caring and commitment to new perceptions is essential in today's shifting business environment. To elevate beyond our BVI's, we have to be centered in love, not our opinions. Favorite quote about this: "Love is higher than opinion. If people love one another the most varied opinions can be reconciled—thus one of the most important tasks for humankind today and in the future is that we should learn to live together and understand one another. If this human fellowship is not achieved, all talk of development is empty."—Rudolf Steiner

Key signals in today's global economy show just how difficult it is to run and scale a corporation. Consider the following:

- Business models are changing rapidly. If you don't pay attention to the competition, you put your business at risk. Today the average S&P 500 company stays on the list for just 18 years, down from 60 years in the 1950s.
- There are 28.8M small businesses (those with fewer than 500 employees) with 56.8M employees. These firms account for 99.7 percent of all businesses. Only one-third of these will survive 10 years from now.2
- Technology is forcing corporations to innovate at an unprecedented pace. To truly innovate, everyone must focus on questions that enable innovation. If we stay stuck in our BVIs, we will be resistant to the signals which means we will stop innovating in our thinking.
- Value Creation today is very different. In the past, 80 percent of value was in tangible assets but today, 80 percent of value is in intangible assets such as knowledge.

CM: It isn't the products that matter. For your corporation to flourish, you need a process that drives the quest for driving past the BVIs and Assumptions. The more your corporation can focus on new perspectives, the more progress will be generated. Knowledge is energy and the more energy you have will lead to more innovative thoughts.

Some other Cauliflower Moments of decision-making assumptions:

Signal: The annual budgeting process again...

CM: Annual budgeting process creates Silos and fractured alignment. Groups start protecting what is "theirs." The traditional annual budgeting and planning process is broken and full of flaws. It's too complex, includes assumptions that often turn out to be wrong, and doesn't respond well to a volatile and competitive world. It's stressful for company leaders who have to endure endless budget iterations, debate over conflicting business goals, and sandbagging, all of which lead to poor decision-making. The result is a final product that becomes less relevant with each passing month.

We need to redefine this process. Start with the wisdom of what needs to be accomplished. What is the truth that your company needs to be focused on? Then set quarterly goals and drive quickly to fail and keep questioning.

Signal: The Lead Generation process isn't driving bottom-line results.

CM: Siloed goals drive self-centered accomplishment. What is the goal? All departments in the company are either in sales or sales support. Leads are about the sales–support operations that drive revenue to happen. The Demand Generation marketing team is generating leads and hitting its goal, but the sales team isn't hitting its revenue numbers. The Demand team is locked into BVIs, believing its job is done because it passed the leads to sales while the sales team feels it doesn't have the leads to hit the numbers. But the company loses because the revenue number isn't hit.

If you react from the BVI layer, you would go focus on sales; however, by questioning and getting to the truth, you could potentially find out that your leads weren't really the leads you needed to win.

Signal: Revenue isn't ramping up the way you want.

CM: You aren't hitting your revenue targets so you need more leads. From the BVI layer, the reaction would be to ask marketing for more leads. Taking a Questioning approach, you might consider whether there are problems with sales presentation, pricing, target audience, whether trade show leads provide better leads than an email campaign, and so on.

Signal: Employer behavior isn't what you were expecting.

Decision-making isn't in the team's best interest and self-centered actions are happening. People are playing the politics game, not the "I care" game.

CM: You have set your values, but people aren't acting in line with the corporate values. You have to go deeper. Empower the people to seek improving knowledge. Drive a philosophy of the corporation operating on caring and certainty. Growth of knowledge directly equates to economic growth.

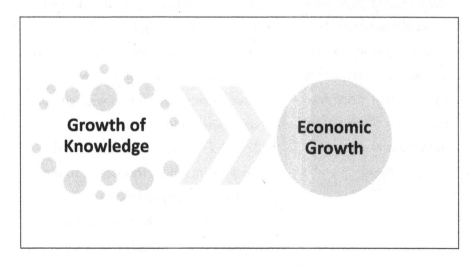

Some employee decisions that depict the BVIs in which people are stuck include:

- Your behavior doesn't hurt others so you can act how you want to act.
- Expense reports: You think you are justified in buying the overpriced bottle of wine, taking the costlier flight, renting the most expensive car, slipping in an extra receipt, and so forth. In your mind, nobody cares and everybody does it. You believe your needs are more important than the company's.

At the BVI layer, an employee feels justified, but at the questioning layer, you should be asking why you feel these expenses are necessary. Are you unhappy at work and this masks it? Are you trying to feel bigger and more important than you really are? Are you creating an Illusion of the reality you so desperately want?

- The truth is that your decisions are hurting others and you are putting your priorities ahead of your colleagues and the company overall. Don't fool yourself; people know. Your finance team knows, your HR team knows, and the execs know.
- Ask yourself what kind of wake you want to leave behind. Just like a boat traveling through water, you can leave a big wake or small ripple. Your actions have a similar impact on your employer or business and your reputation.
- So, what can you do to improve the decision-making processes in your team and your corporation?
- Put the needs of the corporation and others before yourself.

A great example of this is shown in the following scenario. I went to an ex-boss and said I needed another headcount to do x, y, and z. He said no. We then locked ourselves into a debate and he finally said, "Instead of flying business class, fly coach and you will have your money to hire your person." A *wow* moment. It sounds so simple, but I was so locked into my BVIs, assuming I deserved to fly business class, I *needed* to fly business class, and I liked how I felt flying business class. But, the funny thing was, it was all fake. I slept most of the time anyway. I stopped focusing on myself, saved the money, hired the person, and drove another $10 million in revenue.

Some business operations illusions to be aware of:

- In the SAAS (Software as a Service) world, first year renewals are like a mirage; we have a 99 percent retention rate, we are amazing, and then at year three, renewals fall off a cliff. Why? Because you believed the illusion that you must be amazing because so many people renew in year one but the truth is, it is human biology. People will renew in year two still hoping that their decision was correct because they don't want to admit it was wrong. But, at year three, they will pull the plug.
- Employee turnover is low so we must be great, but our growth has slowed and we are missing our numbers. The BVI is that your pay may be too high, everybody may be performing at a low level, and you don't have enough accountability to drive results so everybody is comfortable and nothing is happening
- Sales is hitting its numbers, but it is taking more and more leads to deliver the results. The BVI is that you are hitting your numbers; the signal is the leads required to do so are sky rocketing and the model isn't scalable.

The bulk of issues that we encounter in business are a result of people focusing on their version of reality. We stay too busy to stop and truly question. The BVIs make decisions easy, but unasked questions lead to a reality that doesn't meet expectations.

Signals: Listen for the assumptions around all areas of decisions in your organization.

- Do you see employees on your teams or in your organization making self-decisions?
- Your behavior matters. Remain centered and non-judgmental. Stay in the what you know, not what you think you know.
- Don't let circumstances, peer pressure, materialism, insecurities, or conventional wisdom bury you from asking questions that lead to better decisions.
- Don't be too busy to ask inside-out questions.
- Ask better questions
- Don't ask why something did or didn't happen. Instead, ask what you need to learn from this experience.
- Ask what the intention of your decision is.
- Make sure you are focused on the core of what is known compared to what you thought was known.

Keep in Mind the Big Three Signals

- **Desire:** Strong influence of founder or senior exec
- **Delay:** Teams are worried about failure
- **Defense:** Bad decisions don't get reversed

CHAPTER 3

The Basics Matter: Upgrading the Human Experience

The results we get in our lives and in our work aren't the result of the most recent action; they are the sum of all the repeated actions that have taken place over time.

To change your approach to work, you must free yourself from established rules and entrenched ideas about work and the workplace. The Boxes of Limitations around the workplace are many. In this chapter, we will look at some of the signals around people, policies, and procedures in our enterprises and highlight ways to break out of the BVIs we have constructed.

Allowing your company and its employees to have the freedom to break out of the conventional way of evaluating outcomes to evaluating the signals with new points of view is essential. If we don't train our thoughts, if we don't pay attention to the basics of people, policies, and procedures, we will be ruled by impulses and by moment-to-moment circumstances. Bringing a unity of direction allows an order and harmony to be developed in the organization. Everyone's performance is tightly coupled to the system in which they work. Good performances are an extension of how people feel.

Unity of Direction does not mean a still and fixed environment. It means creating an environment where systematic questioning is always present. You should aim to create an organization that is wide awake, always moving towards a unified conclusion. Keep in mind that the BVIs have varying degrees of challenge to change. The BVIs and the assumptions they drive tend to lead us toward overlooking significant information. Instead, we need to be driving a logic process that systematically drives questions and a march towards evidence. The consequences of decisions derived from our BVIs, rather than from evidence, are significant.

I learned this early at our company when I tried to incorporate a Business Intelligence data tool too early and we didn't adopt it. What people really needed at that point was a way either to get more resources or have fewer things on their plate. Instead, I was trying to drive data visibility, but we had no resources to devote to it and so it failed.

As managers and employees, we need to drive to evidence. Focusing on the signals around the people, policies, and procedures and developing a framework to help people drive towards evidence mindsets is vital.

It is important to look deeper at how a Belief, Value, or Illusion is formed.

Beliefs

What are the main sources of errors in our beliefs? We have given up traditional searching as a means to driving our beliefs. Today, searching means Google. Consider Google's mission: The main *purpose of Google Search* is to hunt for text in publicly accessible documents. This doesn't say the information is the truth; it is just information. We need to conduct the kind of searching that past generations did: searching for facts. Common opinions of our friends, family, and advertising now rule. Changing someone's beliefs involves creating a culture of knowledge that isn't believed or disbelieved; it is to be listened to without bias. The basis for all beliefs needs to be deliberately sought, not carelessly accepted. You want beliefs based on evidence, not suggestions.

Values

Values relate to our imagination and stories. In our corporations, we are striving for the unity of direction. What somebody values, they will excel at. We need to drive an environment that moves people from the stories they create to a sequence of knowledge that helps them establish values based on a firm basis of reason. The strong cultural values in your company and the way your leaders are living according to these values will move your employees to valuing what the company values. The more our corporate values can be held up as valid truths accessible to us all, the more they give employees the ability to create curiosity around the evidence.

Illusions

These are rampant in our society today but, in fact, they are the easiest to change. Today, we let the end desire control the process of thinking and finding the facts. The power of suggestions hijacks the process. An example is found in today's advertising, which gives you all the reasons why you have a problem and then you're given a suggested solution. In 30 seconds, the advertisers have manufactured a problem and presented a solution. If you don't search further, you will be propelled into actions that may or may not be appropriate for you.

At work, you must drive your unity of direction and create a culture of IEEE—Information, to Experiments, to Experience, to Epiphany. Testing each Illusion with a process that takes the information, runs an experiment, has an experience and then has epiphanies is key to making decisions on conclusions drawn from evidence. As a manager, your goal should be to make your corporation an experience of seeking IEEE processes. They are better than any Illusion could ever be!

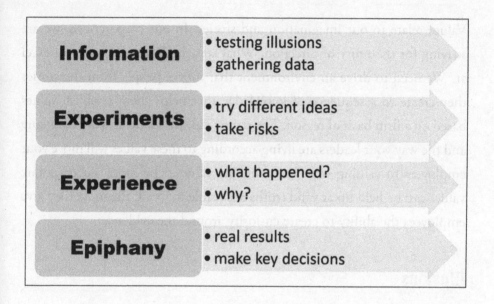

Information	• testing illusions • gathering data
Experiments	• try different ideas • take risks
Experience	• what happened? • why?
Epiphany	• real results • make key decisions

Testing the signals coming from your employees, executives, meetings, and behavior issues is vital. You should always be wondering what is driving the signal and from what part of BVI is in the Box of Limitations.

Is this signal a Belief issue?

Is this signal a Value issue?

Is this signal an Illusion?

Knowing which type of signal you are getting helps you determine follow-up action and how hard it will be to get the employee to open up to questioning to get the truth and having a Cauliflower Moment (CM).

Example of a Belief Signal:

Signal: Employee productivity is suffering.

CM: It is scientifically proven that weekly performance coaching and goals is an effective timeframe to drive increased performance in your organization. Imagine if you questioned your beliefs on optimum brain performance for your employees and you found out that by providing weekly performance check-ins and recaps, you could drive a 2x increase in people's performance? Having a strong performance rhythm to your culture can make a radical difference in the effectiveness of your teams.

Today's world is a noisy place and just like in the wild, knowing which signals to pay attention to is essential. Knowing which BVI signals to pay attention to may not be a life-or-death matter as it is in the wild but it is critical to the success in organizations and life. Listening for signals spans feedback not only on products but also from employees, customers, and your organization.

Building teams is similar to acting. The trust needed to generate amazing performances from our teams every day amounts to getting past the false BVIs and getting knowledge into a solid automated and reliable system. We have to drive trust and clarity to enable those performances to manifest.

In discussing organizational development, I often use a sports analogy. In baseball, you have a second baseman playing for the Giants who bats third in the rotation. The player is hitting .220 and fans hate him so the player is traded to the Yankees, where he bats sixth and hits .290. Why? Did the person change? Or was it the environment in which he worked?

In a recent Talent Portability Study, Boris Groysberg showed that of 1,052 rock star employees who changed jobs, 50 percent of the employees did poorly in the year following the job switch, and they never recovered. Why? Talent performance is tightly connected to teams, projects, and culture.

Helping people discover their insights helps people to perform at their greatest potential. Most people have the ability to execute but they need direction to reach their peak.

Key signals around people and policies in an organization:

Signal: Lack of attention to details.
CM: Managers drive effectiveness. To have effective teams, paying attention to the details in every aspect is critical. Create a team environment that thrives on the habit of testing BVIs and moves past guesses and opinions to mental discipline around not overlooking significant inputs.

Signal: Lack of clear direction.
CM: I often see companies and leaders stuck in their BVIs and not basing decisions on the truth. A leader's role is to help the teams and the company by providing deliberate and intentional insights. Operating on untruths, judgements, biases, and prejudices lead to an organization which is no longer thinking. Clear direction leads to a healthy way of gaining knowledge which leads to big ideas.

Signal: Doubting people's decisions and information.
CM: When we doubt, we destroy the IEEE process. Doubt is subtle and shows up in the Illusion of constructive questioning, questions like "…says who" or "I will do something if…" are questions designed to create the shadow of doubt. This Illusion of authentic questioning takes away the confidence, faith, resolve, and vision and replaces these qualities with uncertainty, confusion, inertia, insecurity, and fear. We need to move past a culture of doubting to a culture of having the will and desire to find

out. Igniting people's thinking is a key operating objective and we must be careful not to kill the creative energy with doubt.

Create the breeding ground for IEEE processes on every signal that comes in. You should have the wish to question and grow in wisdom and in life.

> *"King Solomon tells us that only a fool believes everything; the wise man submits everything to intelligent inquiry before committing himself. Questioning is a path towards growth in wisdom and life."*

Signal: Toxic Employee Behavior

Employers often have problems caused by ignoring toxic behavior or being fascinated with superstars. Sometimes these two issues are present in the same employee. The bottom line is that if you don't break past the BVIs and question the costs of these employees' behaviors, your organization will falter. Your team is watching, listening, and seeing how a difficult employee is handled.

Key Signals to watch for include:
- Do you have a superstar who can't get along with your other teams?
- Are your teams starting to isolate themselves from one another to avoid the conflict?
- Do you have a culture where the fascination with a superstar doesn't take into account the circumstances that allow that individual to excel?

Underestimating the impact of a toxic employee has a bigger impact than you realize and can divide organizations and demoralizes teams.

Signal: A lack of politeness.

CM: Nobody has ever been fired for being too polite. Every thought and every action deserves politeness. You can't have a culture of, "you are wrong, I am right." Each thought pushes the collective thinking forward and contributes the ever-growing wisdom and understanding. Driving for tolerance, openness, and politeness for all thoughts contributes to an enterprise that will have a scaling energy equation.

Signal: People stuck in their BVIs.

CM: You can't have a culture of employees sticking to their views or world views. Push your teams to reach for insights beyond their BVIs. It isn't about what you know; it is about the meaning of what you know that really matters. You are trying to ignite the potential in each person. Potential is untapped energy that can push the enterprise forward.

Signal: A corporation is stuck in its own world.

You are overvaluing what you think you know which manifests in thinking you know exactly what every employee and every customer wants.

CM: Judgement is at the root of this problem. You have to refrain from judgement at all costs. Freeing your company and your actions from judgement opens you up to the world of knowledge.

Signal: Leaders often make statements as if they are facts and because they are in power, people will just accept the statements.

CM: Author and leadership expert Michael Hyatt once said, "Make sure people know the difference in everything you say…the difference between what you know and what you think you know."

The false BVIs of things you think you know creates distrust, insecurity, and vulnerability. Keep things to what you know and process your questions around knowing more.

Common Signals around this idea are:

Have you ever walked out of a meeting and heard employees saying, "That is way off base?"

Have you ever had a manager overreact to one piece of data and then the feedback loop closes because people are fearful of the reactions?

"We Don't See Things as They Are; We See Them as We Are" is the guiding phrase that I use to drive my BVI questions so that both the company and myself are able to see things as they truly are.

Signal: Technology can save us.

Take the humanness out of the human by driving more and more technology that they are using.

A huge potential downfall in technology is stated well in the book titled *Hooked: How to Build Habit-Forming Products*. The book left me feeling as if there is another attack on our basic humanity. The author says, "Our brains are adapted to seek rewards that make us feel accepted, attractive, important, and included."

CM: We need to realize that technology is designed with motivations other than just helping us. Humans have real physiological limits and dependencies and technology designers know better today exactly how to manipulate these limits.

We need to incorporate the technologies that will help us extend the range of our abilities without limiting our abilities to stay in the moment and maintain the will to find out. We need to employ technologies that drive faster IEEE processes and insight without creating dependencies.

When looking at the overall basics of the enterprise, getting people to be open to new knowledge is vital. "How" it is prepared determines how acceptable it is.

A fun way to think about this is to think about cauliflower; steamed, wasn't very acceptable to me, but when mashed, it is amazing, and with Alfredo sauce, delicious. Truly, the "how" it was prepared was what really mattered.

It is astounding to me how locked people are to their BVIs. I see it daily in our organization and other companies. I also see it in life in general. As I have been challenging everything with the BVI construct, I force people and teams to address their BVIs. It plays out in so many situations. For example, we hear from customers that they want this feature or they need this product, and our internal reaction is, "Oh, why would they want that? That is not their job!" WOW! Our BVIs say that they should never want that feature in our product. But the market is telling us they do. Will we listen and actually understand? Or will we just do what we want to do?

Another example on the personal front concerns vitamin C. The tremendous power of vitamin C in high doses has been well documented. However, much of the media doesn't share this opinion which shows how we face biases in our daily life. In spite of the media's skepticism, I researched the use of vitamin C when I was looking for ways to improve my effectiveness. I started a regimen of 12,000 mg a day two years ago and 25,000 mg blasts every 2 hours whenever I started to feel sick. Guess what? In three years, I have never been sick and haven't had to see a doctor. Imagine the productivity boost to enterprises if you could cut down employee sick days by 50 percent just by doing this? Yet, when I try to show people how effective vitamin C can be, they are very skeptical. They don't believe it can be that powerful even though I am living proof because it's not what they have been led to believe and they refuse to ask important questions: What more do I need to know? Where did my BVIs come from? Run the Information, Experiments, Experience, and Epiphany process the next time you feel sick. What do you have to lose?

Some Signals Around Procedures

Signal: Have you ever examined why companies have trouble at certain scaling points?

CM: The common assumption is that companies have to evolve when they have between 100 to 160 employees, then again when they reach 300 employees, and then again at 1,000 employees I thought this reasoning was related to technology or systems. But, after researching it more closely, I found out about the Dunbar Limit theory.

Robin Dunbar, a professor of evolutionary psychology at Oxford University said, "Brain size correlates to group size." He studied the behavior of primates compared to humans and figured out that humans can handle up to 148 connections. Beyond this, the communication and coordination demand outstrips what the human mind can handle. The bigger then number, the more you have to filter; the more you filter, the less effective you become.

I have seen this theory proven at many of the companies where I've worked. At one company earlier in my career, we hit the wall at $100 million in revenue. We couldn't scale beyond it. We treaded water for three years, and then the company was sold. The company was log jammed at the top; there was a very small team of founders and the span of control never expanded.

You have probably heard there are people suited for start-ups and there are people suited for large companies. It boils down to our ability to pay attention. We can maintain more ties at the expense of weaker connections for each relationship.

Since our brain, specifically the neocortex, hasn't changed in hundreds of years, the limits of our attention and time resources remain the same. Therefore, when we maintain more relationships, each one will get a smaller piece of the attention pie. Since the strength of a relationship is directly related to the amount of time and attention devoted to it, this usually leads to a weaker relationship (though not always, because there are other components of a relationship such as intensity, trust, and reciprocity). The important question we should be asking is whether or not we can get by with weaker relationships.

To scale your company and your employees, you need to understand the impact of scaling capacity. You can layer in technology to try and drive past the basic human limits, but doing this will be at the expense of weaker relationships. In today's corporations, it is essential that you focus on building trust which suggests stronger relationships. Pay attention to the Dunbar Limit and drive scaling capacity: Scaling capacity = the number of connections compared to strength of connections (managers/employees). The cognitive processing power of our brains is fundamentally still the same as it was centuries ago.

People have trouble scaling because they want to keep control, but they can't maintain this control when the enterprise gets larger. They start to filter, people start to lose direction, and performance suffers.

Other Signals Around Dunbar Limits
- A manager who doesn't want to let go of his or her direct involvement in a task or issue.

- A team that isn't growing its output because the manager is unable to give the team the necessary direction.

CM: There is a real limit to human physiology that explains why people need to let go of the control and scale their companies. Understanding this concept helps them understand they aren't dysfunctional.

Ways to apply the Dunbar Limit principle in the enterprise:
- How many direct reports on a team should report to a manager?
- How many employees should report to a founder? Scaling past the Dunbar Limit is a critical time for a company.
- What are the purposes of any technology you deploy? Is it to help your team scale past the Dunbar Limit?

Productivity

Signal: Are your employees struggling to keep up? Do you ever hear people say, "I spend all of my time in meetings and have no time to get work done?"

CM: This isn't only an issue for your company. In 2016, a *Harvard Business Review* study showed time spent by workers collaborating with colleagues has increased by 50 percent over the last 20 years. Additionally, about 80 percent of a worker's time is spent on collaborative activities including reading and writing emails, making and answering phones, and attending online or in person meetings.

You need to create an onsite culture and remote culture that is appropriate for your workplace. According to Global Workplace Analytics, 36 percent of employees would choose working from home over a pay raise. Free from distractions, productivity goes up. The key to getting the job done remotely is all about having the right technology and clearly aligned goals. Companies and organizations that commit to remote work can expect happier employees and more efficient teams.

Finding People Who Fit

Signal: How much are you investing in your hiring process? Is it comparable to what you are investing in the new customer acquisition process or other areas of the organization?

CM: This is a bigger topic, and chapter 4 is devoted to the assumptions and the re-crafting of ways to improve this process.

Onboarding

Signal: Are people showing up for their first day of work and their workspace and managers aren't ready for them?

CM: Misguided assumptions abound in this area of the employee journey. For me, the deep questioning came from thinking about how to accomplish the following goals:

- Drive 2x productivity by effecting onboarding.
- Decrease turnover. The stats on turnover are scary—20 percent of new hires leave within 48 days, and 40 percent of new leaders fail within 18 months.
- Decrease time to productivity/proficiency. What we have done in our process to create success and higher probability of high performance?
- Create a trusting environment. We want all new employees to feel part of the team from Day 1.

- Create focus and alignment with company goals and objectives. We use the Objectives and Key Results (OKR) process to drive clarity of goals and performance. This process was developed by Andy Grove at Intel and is now used by many leading companies.
- Clear alignment with Metrics used to evaluate performance. We drive these metrics from the OKR process and a series of questions on our weekly check-in processes. See Appendix A for the questions we use.
- We make it fun. We send a welcome kit with shirts and other items to new employees' homes the week before they're starting to ease their entry into the company and help them feel more relaxed. We have mugs, shirts, and information sheets waiting at their desks.

Other Signals that you might have problems with onboarding:
- Are employees leaving within two months? What are your retention statistics?
- What is your success rate on new managers? Do you have a retention rate of 60 percent or better at 18 months?

Some questions you should ask in your organization, regardless of its size:
- Who drives your onboarding strategy? Is there executive involvement?
- Have you crafted your new employees' experiences?
- What are your defined goals for the employee onboarding?
- What is a new employee's first day like? First week? First month?

Signals Around Facilities

Do you pay enough attention to the details? Everything about your location and office sends a signal.

We recently moved to a newer upgraded office. All the alterations were completed but we ignored a dirty ceiling tile until a candidate came in and made a comment about the stain on one of them! We were ignoring the signal, but to the potential employee, the dirty tile sent a message about our company. We got the tile fixed quickly.

You need to look more closely at your office set-up.

Signal: Are people sitting in the area that enables them to be most productive?

We tend to sit people in areas we think are right, without considering what helps the person be the most productive. Some people need quiet areas, some like noise, other like light, and some like dark.

CM: Are we maintaining a clean inviting building? Care for the building = care for the people in it. Are your chairs comfortable? Is the lighting right? What is the noise level? Do you have fun?

Question everything. Don't assume that just because something has been in place for a while, it is good or appropriate. Ask for input and value the information you receive.

In our organization, we strive to get employee feedback on everything related to our office. We get feedback via manager weekly check-ins and weekly executive meetings with People Operations, as well as from comment boxes, and so on. Each employee is a vital part of the company, with a unique role and experience. Your job is to create the correct system that will allow everyone to reach their full potential and help them discover their insights.

The people, policies, and procedure basics allow you to fortify your company against the natural tendencies of human nature. The basics allow you to have a process for each function in your enterprise that is aimed at discovering the facts and established decisions based on a firm basis of reason. Security, trust, and creativity will blossom and people will deliver great performances.

Key Takeaways

- Have you created an environment that has a clear unity of direction?
- Driving for an IEEE (Information, to Experiments, to Experience, to Epiphanies) process on each signal that comes in unlocks the potential within your organizations and your people.
- Know your signal types as they come in: Is it a signal about Belief, Value, or Illusion?
- Thinking and processes don't just happen; they have to be provoked! Most people have the talent to execute, they just need some direction.
- Keep your company in the sweet spot of focusing on the will to find out.

CHAPTER 4
Finding Employees Who Fit

To compete successfully today, you need to have structured processes that define your organization in all areas. The odyssey of hiring the right employees led me to develop a three-pronged strategy including: Unity, Freedom, and Clarity.

As we were scaling, I was constantly getting signals about how our process wasn't working. For example:

- The majority of our managers had little time to focus on finding new employees.
- With poorly defined business outcomes, interviewers weren't clear on which candidates to seek and consequently received too many and inappropriate résumés.
- Interviewers went into appointments without knowing who the candidate was or without having seen a résumé.
- Casual feedback, manifested in a thumbs-up or thumbs-down between interviewers in the hallway, was the rule of rating.

In addition, companies lacking a standardized process are five times more likely to make a bad hire that costs, on average, $11,000. However, contrary to popular belief, technical skills are not the primary reason why new hires fail. Instead, poor interpersonal skills dominate the list, and many managers admit they overlooked these flaws during the job interview process.

Common signals about interviewers and the mistakes they make:

- Most people overvalue first impressions and personality.
- People believe that they can change somebody.

Common Signals Why New Hires Fail

According to a Leadership IQ Study, 26 percent of new hires fail because they can't accept feedback, 23 percent because they're unable to understand and manage emotions, 17 percent because they lack the necessary motivation to excel, 15 percent because they have the wrong temperament for the job, but only 11 percent because they lack the necessary technical skills.

We find employees via referrals, recruiters, websites, acquisitions, and so on, with each of these sources having a unique success rate that provides useful information. For our company, paid search for key positions and referrals are by far the top two ways to find higher probability matches. It makes sense: people who love our team, values, and quest for innovative thinking, refer their friends and, most likely, these people will have the same inner constitution to become successful employees.

As I looked back on our process and our ability to scale, a top signal for me revolved around Unity and the Energy created in the company.

Signal: I had to come to the realization that the system of unity we were trying to create was really all about energy.

CM: I went back to my engineering background and thought of our company in terms of one of the Laws of Thermodynamics.

Thermodynamics is the study of the interrelation between heat, work, and internal energy of a system. It is a great way to understand the bigger picture of what is happening in our lives and organizations.

- You cannot win (that is, you cannot get something for nothing because matter and energy are conserved).
- You cannot break even (you cannot return to the same energy state because there is always an increase in disorder; entropy always increases).
- You cannot get out of the game (because absolute zero is unattainable).

One of the four main laws of Thermodynamics states that Energy can neither be created nor destroyed; it can only change forms. In any process, total energy in the universe remains the same. So, when you're searching to hire employees, you should think about the energy you are creating and how the new people you're adding to the system help you balance the energy equation in your favor. The positive potential of a team with unity of direction and purpose.

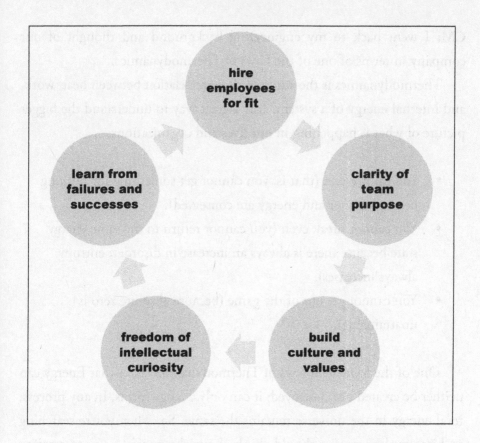

In the natural world view, everything is formed into societies. Our countries, religions, corporations, and bodies are all societies. The human body is a society of cells organized into collaborative groups. Each cell behaves in a socially responsible manner by resting, dividing, or dying as needed for the good of the body. In an organizational society, we are looking for the same traits. We want to bring people into the society who will work in a socially responsible manner with the unity we are trying to create.

"Hire for will, train for skill" What is the will? This means what people know is less important than who they are. What you are changes but who you are, doesn't!

Clarity comes into the science of the hiring process. As we were redefining our process, I was influenced by the book *Work Rules* by Lazlo Bock. We needed to redefine our process around a key notion and I kept Bock's view in mind. He said, "The goal of our interview process is to predict how candidates will perform once they join the team. We achieve that goal by doing what the science says: combining behavioral and situational structured interviews with assessments of cognitive ability, conscientiousness, and leadership."

The science of interviewing stresses several important factors:

- Most interview outcomes are determined in the first 10 seconds. Tricia Prickett and Neha Gada-Jain, two psychology students at the University of Toledo, collaborated with their professor Frank Bernieri and from a study conducted in 2000, they determined that judgments made in the first 10 seconds of an interview could predict the outcome of the interview.
- The structure of a job interview determines its effectiveness to finding the right candidate fit. In 1998, Frank Schmidt and John Hunter published a meta-analysis of 85 years of research on how well various assessments predict performance. They looked at 19 different assessment techniques and found that typical, unstructured job interviews were poor at predicting how someone would perform once he or she was hired. Unstructured interviews have an ability to predict accurately only 14 percent of an employee's performance in the job and a 14 percent chance of an employee fitting your company's needs.
- The top two assessment techniques as proven in the study were: 29 percent work sample tests and 26 percent structured

interviews, where candidates are asked a consistent set of questions with clear criteria to assess the quality of responses. There are two kinds of structured interviews: behavioral and situational.

- Behavioral interviews ask candidates to describe prior achievements and match those to what is required in the current job (i.e., "Tell me about a time...?"). Situational interviews present a job-related hypothetical situation (i.e., "What would you do if...?").

Key Signals Around Clarity of the Candidates

Signal: Is caring a vital part of who/what they are?

CM: Caring isn't a weakness. Someone who cares is someone who will overcome obstacles and will thrive even in a constantly changing environment. Someone who cares will not let authority dictate his or her BVIs; he or she will have the energy and courage to question beyond opinions.

Signal: Do they love themselves?

CM: Self-love is almost a taboo phrase because it is considered narcissism. In fact, self-love is fulfillment, joy, and the ability to share love. When people don't love themselves, they will try to get love in unhealthy ways and will then exhibit types of behaviors such as selfishness, overindulging, or blaming others. Self-love drives systematic questioning that awakens people to the truth. If you don't love yourself, you won't question for fear of the truth.

> I realized, for many years, I hadn't loved myself. I looked at everything that was wrong with me, and it made me a bad employee. I was selfish, I overindulged, I blamed, and I looked for love/reassurance in all the wrong places. I was completely focused on myself and this reflected the way I treated others. Gradually, I learned to accept and love myself and realize that I was made just the way I am supposed to be. Gaining this awareness gave me the desire to systematically question everything.

Ways to Evaluate Whether Self-Love Is Present
- How potential candidates dress shows that they care about themselves.
- They take care of themselves physically for health, not vanity.
- They control destructive behavior.
- They can handle failure.
- They value themselves.
- They aren't afraid to lead.

You must allow employees and potential employees the freedom in the process to really explore all sides. Consider some of the following signals to ensure freedom from your BVIs to allow you to see the reality of the person talking with you.

Signal: Are Comfort, Conformance, and Convenience driving your decisions in the evaluation process?
CM: Society pushes us to Comfort, Conformance, and Convenience. However, you can't let these be the guiding pressures when you're trying to find great team members. Intention and presence have to be your focus. You must dig deeper to get past the Illusions and evaluate the whole person.

Signal: Be proud of your company's Values and talk freely about how they shape how your teams work together.

CM: You can never amplify your values too much. Get your company's key values visible and at the forefront. You want to hire people who want to join your cause.

Signal: Are you making your decisions based on the first 90 seconds?

We were running so fast and winging our interviews that we were relying on first impressions to dictate our hiring processes.

CM: It's true that you can determine a lot in the first 90 seconds after you meet someone but you have to get beyond these first impressions. Eighty percent of managers said they decided on a hire in the first 90 seconds of meeting someone.

Psychologists call this behavior "Thin Slicing," and researchers think this behavior is a survival mechanism that we have developed to quickly decide if someone is friend or foe. The important things decided in those first few seconds include whether someone is trustworthy, smart, successful, and so on.

We have to drive for objective evaluations and not let our first 90 seconds determine our decision. An intention to develop a trained process for the organization will allow you to run your processes without reactions to impulses, biases, or judgements.

Consider the following when you're making a hiring decision:
- Hear all the facts before you make a decision.
- Use evidence, not emotions to make your decisions. We all want the freedom to think what we want to think, but true freedom is the power to have trained power of thought.

- Divide and conquer to systematize bias out of the selection process. We assign each person on the interviewing team a role in the process to "own." During the debriefing session, everyone shares their evidence. This way the team makes the hiring decision and neutralizes the emotional bias of each team member.
- Look at each interview as not an interview, but as a journey you are going to take to appreciate and discover the other person with no judgement.
- Interviewers make mistakes by overvaluing the quality of the candidate's first impression, level of assertiveness, affability, and communication skills. Mistakes are also made if the interviewer is overly confident in his or her own interviewing skills or uses cloudy judgment such as assuming attending a prestigious university or technical brilliance is a prerequisite or predictor of success.

Signal: Freedom in this process also comes to play in one of those life-lesson ways… Cheap isn't always a good thing!
I thought I learned this lesson already but I kept making this mistake over and over again. When I bought my first set of garden tools for my first house, I was so proud of how inexpensive the rake, hoe, and shovel were. Then, my father came over and laughed about how cheaply these tools were made. Well, within two weeks, the head of the rake was off, the shovel was broken, and I was back at the hardware store buying quality tools!

You should never hire cheap because you don't have the money. We made decisions to hire based on hiring someone whom we could afford rather than the right person for the job. We have had about an 80 percent failure rate with these hires.

CM: When you're ramping up your company, you may well be short of available funds. No matter how alluring it is, you are sacrificing something when you hire someone for below market rates. Don't let your policies or your financial situation prevent you from hiring exceptional people.

Don't fall for the overqualified person who is willing to work for much less than he or she was earning before. This is an illusion that won't last. The person may join your company but within three to six months, he will feel as if he is working harder than he expected and now wants compensation at his old level.

We had to rewrite our interviewing process. First, we asked the following series of questions:

- Do you/and or your team really know how to interview a candidate?
- Are you the kind of interviewer who talks about how great the company is and how everyone gets on well with each other, and how amazing the offices are?
- Do you properly probe the candidate's experience and capabilities?
- Have you ever been formally and professionally trained on how to conduct an effective interview?

After asking these questions, we found that most of our team had no interview training and simply did them in the same style in which they had been interviewing.

Systematic Hiring Issues That We Addressed

Signal: Hit-and-Run Hiring

I have made this mistake more than once. I was so excited at getting a new employee onboard, which allowed me to attack the 20 other burning fires. Somehow, we expected the new hire just to handle his or her job without providing any guidance…and it always resulted in less than desired results.

Consider the following examples:

- Your child turns 16 and you get her a car but never teach her how to drive. You just expect she would know how.
- You hire a senior executive assuming he knows how to operate in your company. Don't assume that is the case. Set the person up to win, and you'll find any of his weaknesses in the first quarter.

CM: Don't walk away from new hires thinking they have it. This has been a painful lesson I have had to relearn time and again. We tend to hire and think thank God, now on to the next issue, but, you have to stay connected and help them succeed. Find their weaknesses and manage to those.

Interview Preparation Process

Our Process

In our hiring process, there were several goals in mind when we undertook an examination of our process.

- To scale the company, a large number of people had to be recruited.

- The metrics that we chose to measure our success in this process by were, to beat the industry averages on retention of employees after 90 days and after 2 years.
- To create a great candidate experience that treated all candidates fairly with no biases and or prejudices.

To accomplish these goals, we had to:

- Take our hiring process out of the first-impression hiring reaction. As explained previously with regards to general scaling, we had to understand some basic human limits. The brain is like a committee of experts. All the parts of the brain work together, but each part has its own special properties. We needed our process to work in a similar fashion.
- Observe all interactions. How somebody treats your teams is critical. Every step from the phone screens to the email communications to how they treat the front desk at check-in matters.
- A hiring committee is formed for each job. Each person on the committee of employees in the process has a defined purpose. We interview for the following traits:
  - ▶ **Job Fit:** Sometimes this includes a work sample test, depending on the role. At other times, it is simple dialogue and questioning.
  - ▶ **Team Fit:** Led by a team member of the team they are joining. We are looking at energy, the questioning process, and personality fit.
  - ▶ **Culture Fit:** Usually conducted by somebody in our people operations team, we're trying to get a consistent view of

whether the prospective employee fits our values, energy, and pursuits.

- Feedback is essential and required. We use a technology tool—an applicant tracking system (ATS)—to simplify our ability to gather the information necessary to have enough knowledge to make evidence-based decisions.
  Selection is a team selection process so no one vote means more than another. There has to be a unanimous vote before an offer is extended, even if the process is delayed and takes longer.

We screen numerous candidates for each role. For executive level positions, it averages more than 200 candidates screened per filled position. This discovery process of driving past the stories and outside influences to a structured process has created a lively, sincere, and more open-minded discipline approached to hiring. Our data proves that it is working.

The secret to a successful interviewing process is to prepare! Be clear on exactly what you want to get out of the meeting. As they say "past performance is usually a good indicator of future performance" so taking a good look at what people have achieved in their career will help you. We meet as a team before the interviews and the manager describes what he or she is looking for and what tradeoffs the manager might make, such as less experience, a person from our exact market, or what other specifics are required.

How things are prepared determines how well they are accepted.

We spend dedicated time on our Core Values to see how candidates align. In our company, the three essential Core Values are:

Love

Passion

Innovation/Intellectual Curiosity

The first two are pretty self-evident, but the third trait requires some explanation.

Intellectual Curiosity

When I'm speaking to candidates, chances are they have already been extensively vetted. They probably have the skills and experience required for the position, and they fit our work culture. As a result, there is not much to be gained by having me test them on these areas. I am looking for people who have the intellectual curiosity predisposition.

I want people who are thoughtful and eager to learn new things, achieve and think beyond the role they're interviewing for, and understand how that role fits into the bigger company picture.

I want to know if they're curious about the business and industry they work in, or if they are simply there to perform their designated role without genuinely understanding what their company does.

We need people who have a desire to realize that they need to deliberately set their BVIs and not just get programed by propaganda. The energy and courage to question is vital to building an enterprise that will scale.

I want to see if they have had the curiosity driven out of them in order to conform. Has their curiosity process been hijacked to be used to compare versus creating, or are they still able to be clever, insightful, and have genuine thoughts?

Key Signals of employees who have had the curiosity programmed out of them:
- Are rigid in their routines
- Stagnant from all the programed instruction

- Distracted by random or trivial things
- Take their BVIs from authority
- Driving curiosity for personal advantage
- Driving curiosity for use in gossip... all the social media sites
- Are obsessed about the fortunes of others

Genuine curiosity to drive and find answers and solutions. *Some key signals and questions around people who have the curiosity traits:*

- People who can and want to grow.
- Diversity of personality, perspective, and background leads to a stronger team. My ultimate target is having intellectually curious people with diverse strengths and perspectives on my team. It all starts with hiring the right people, but it doesn't end there.

Building a team is an ongoing process... but it's a lot easier when you start with the right people.

How to interview for intellectual curiosity

Signal: They must be willing to break the rules sometimes.

A great question to ask is: "Tell me about the last time you broke the rules." You are looking for people who aren't afraid to answer this question.

You're looking for people who knew their purpose/objective. The unity of direction process means they knew their goal, didn't get distracted, and had a steady trend towards completion. You don't need to be rigid in your process, but you need to be rigid in your unity of direction and let the process unfold via testing and questioning. A person who broke the rules to question outside the normal lines of thought with an end in mind is a person who has the curiosity to drive innovation. If someone says he or she never break the rules, then that person is probably too rigid for an environment that is driven by innovation and curiosity.

Signal: Did they think bigger than themselves and their job at their last company?

A question to ask includes: "Did you understand your previous company's challenges? If not, why not?" I find that people who are curious and who care about their companies and industries can grow their roles and become company leaders. I want those people. When interviewing a candidate, be sure to include a few questions that shed light on his or her natural learning patterns.

These questions might include:

- What do you do for fun?
- What books have you read lately?
- How do you learn new things?

When candidates exhibit a strong energy level when explaining answers to any of these questions that is generally a sign of natural curiosity. If they actively seek out new information on a weekly or daily basis, that will be easily reflected in their responses. There is one great rule when it comes to interviewing for intellectual curiosity: if the candidates are asking *you* a lot of questions, they are likely to be intellectually curious. Look for candidates who ask follow-up questions throughout the interview; nearly every candidate will ask questions at the end of the interview, but an intellectually curious individual will likely come up with new questions based on what you are discussing. Their natural interest in the conversation, the factors that go into their role, and the way the company works should all reflect a deeper curiosity.

Fearlessness Is Another Signal of Intellectual Curiosity

Fearlessness is the ability to face a challenging situation head-on with no worry of hurt, harm, or injury, whether that risk is physical, emotional, or mental. If people's trust is in a sure, sound place, they are freer to be fearless. People who aren't afraid to be different naturally stretch boundaries and are often a little weird. A little weirdness goes a long way! An organization that has unity of purpose can have a wide array of individuals all using their unique traits to be successful. Don't let your judgement of their outer appearance cloud your judgement of their abilities.

Key traits around Fearlessness to pick up on in your discussions:
- They are authentic, scared, and vulnerable. They don't hide how they feel. They don't pretend.
- They have learned from failure. They learn from mistakes and try again. There is no reason to be ashamed, embarrassed, or fearful. Failure builds character. It creates epic tales of grand adventure. Failure leads to freedom. Fail your way to success, the sooner, the better.
- They have challenged convention. They are not afraid to go against the grain.
- They speak up. They aren't afraid to be heard, state an opinion, or stake a stand.
- They do what it takes. They take risks.
- They ask for help. They ask someone to mentor them and they ask for direction.

- They trust themselves. They follow through. When you can trust yourself, you're more likely to trust others.
- They learn new skills. They learn to enjoy challenges.
- They don't give up. They try again, brainstorm solutions, or do something different. They look at the problem from a different perspective.

There are many questions that will help you determine whether someone is fearless:

- Ask them about a time they failed and what they did afterwards. You want to see whether the person was chasing a unity of purpose at the time, and wasn't afraid to prove his or her ideas/ thoughts by testing and failing.
- Ask them about a time when they were stuck in a routine and what they did to get out of it?
- Ask about a time they reacted on impulse and it failed?
- Ask about when limited experience misled them to the wrong conclusion?

Last, a signal of an Owner Mentality is vital to them thriving in an environment where Unity, Freedom, and Clarity are in place.

CM: People can be unstoppable because they provide steady, consistent force until an outcome is achieved. Thinking like an owner means people are simultaneously completing tasks reliably while understanding the bigger picture. Employees who are able to think like owners are comfortable with ambiguity and understand how their role impacts and affects others at the company. They bring feedback, insight, and suggestions to every meeting.

They maintain focus and single-minded persistence in spite of obstacles. They exhibit endurance and take the long-term view. Owners are free of the biases of doubt, superstition, and personality.

Ownership Questions to Ask:
- Many obstacles can prevent an organization from achieving its goals; tell me about a time when you met such an obstacle.
- Can you give me an example of a time when you had to solve a really complex problem that required multiple steps across weeks or months?

Driving for Success on Finding Employees that Fit

To create a company where unity, freedom, and clarity can drive your employee choices, you must break from your Box of Limitation around hiring the right people. In today's 24/7 world, impulse decisions often lead to poor hiring decisions. Driving your company's unity of direction and purpose allows your people to truly experience each discussion and determine whether they will enjoy the society you have created. It's essential to develop a process for finding new people that doesn't rely on random or casual interactions, but instead relies on logical, thoughtful questioning.

A process that is intentional and drives the curiosity to learn and know each person keeps your organization from being lost in indifference and illusions.

Key Takeaways

- Is your corporation's unity of direction and purpose understood?
- Do your teams know how to interview?
- Is your interview process defined?
- Take your hiring process out of the first impressions reaction zone.
- The secret is preparation
- Balancing energy in your organization is vital. Each new employee is the positive potential energy that can help balance the Thermodynamics equation of your enterprise.
- Ensure that every people decision is based on a discovery of the facts and conclusions based on these discoveries. Make it an adventure to meet new people and piece together the winning combinations for all parties.

CHAPTER 5

Balancing the Energy Economy of the Enterprise

When looking at the Energy of an Enterprise, I tend to take my cues from nature. In nature, species or individuals that have the largest net energy surplus can dedicate more of their lives to outperforming rivals! At the cellular level, it is proven that gene expression is environmentally influenced. In all things, environmental factors play a vital role. Think in terms of being a composer eliciting amazing performances from musicians and instruments. My goal is to help corporations achieve optimum energy and optimum performance.

Factors that determine the successful energy management of the workplace are the three pillars of energy: the Physical, the Nonphysical, and the Presence. For me, the Laws of Thermodynamics are the base laws of energy that we need to understand. Thermodynamics states that net energy is always the same in the universe and closed systems will suffer increasing entropy over time.

In a corporate setting, entropy can be thought of as the loss of a system's energy to be able to do external work. We want to look at our energy equations of our enterprises to inject as much positive potential energy into our corporations to slow down Entropy and keep our corporations balanced and growing. We will explore how we can look at the signals in each part of the energy equation and tune our systems to maximize the energy equation.

Our job as leaders of organizations, families, and so on is to help people realize what more they need to be questioning. The past president of CBS, Richard Salant, said, "Our job is to give people not what they want, but what we decide they ought to have!" WOW.

We, as leaders, have to think broader. Understanding energy and how to optimize it isn't something people are thinking about, but we can help them realize why they should be interested in learning more.

The Box of Limitations around the Energy Economy of the enterprise is full of BVIs. Energy is at the root of everything. If we don't guide our energy to a trained reaction, we will be driven by impulse and external events. Humans are the only mammals that create their own environments. In today's society, our environments have been overrun with the focus on the wrong things. Properly managing the energy in all your systems, your body, your business, your nutrition, and your environment lead to outcomes that, if managed, can be very positive and if left unmanaged, can be very negative. All organisms must obtain nutrients from their environments to thrive. These nutrients include physical such as light, water, food, and sound and nonphysical such as presence, intention, and no judgment.

A Major CM for me was: We are all focusing on driving for a more connected workplace. More applications, more facilities, and so on but I realized our connection focus is 100 percent incorrect. Connected in a technology sense, resource conservation sense, and so on all distract us from connection to the natural electronics of the universe that we need to help our bodies function at their optimum performance. I had to shift my mindset to maximizing my connection to energy to maximize my performance. I often joke that I have become an "Energitarian." Everything

I consume—and I help our workplace consume—is about maximizing our connection to natural energies and maximizing the thermodynamics equations of the enterprise and life.

Connection to the Physical starts with developing a much broader view of the biological effects of our surroundings. How we make and use energy is all about the light we consume. Each person's energy equation starts with the production of ATP in the body. ATP is Adenosine Triphosphate; it is the energy source for our bodies. We create our own body weight in ATP each day. Two-thirds of the ATP is created by photosynthesis and one-third is from nutrition. So, to get the energy equation right in our employees we need to optimize the ATP production equation! Setting up your facilities and environments for maximizing ATP production is the goal.

A signal that the biological effects of our workplace environments aren't working is:

We are hearing more and more of a new disorder, called Sick Building Syndrome. People are getting sick at the workplace. The environments are affecting health and wellness.

Another signal that our workplace environment is not working is:

Consider this reality: How many companies will celebrate a 10-year anniversary? The Bureau of Labor Statistics states that only 30 percent of companies make it to year 10. If you don't scale your systems to require as little energy as possible to remain in order, it will take more and more energy to maintain order. Eventually, disorder occurs and your business will fail.

Signals Around Physical Energy Drivers

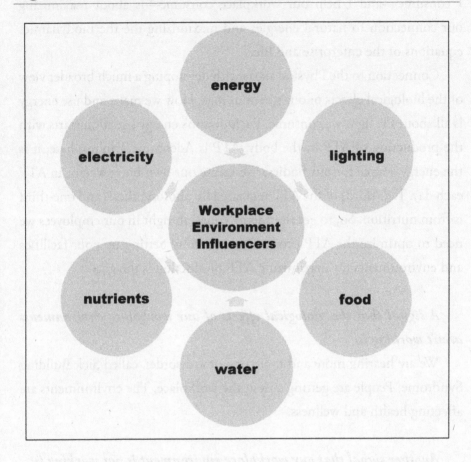

Signal about energy: Do you tend to think of energy as the power your enterprise consumes?
CM: I view the energy equation as creating a Frequency and Vibration of positive energy.

Signal about lighting: What type of lights do you have in the office? Did you just switch to LED?
CM: Planet Earth runs under light energy. Light is critical to the powering of all systems. Under the banner of saving electrical power, we all switched

to LEDs. Little did we realize that LED lights generate a large amount of blue light and have significant health risks. Although we lowered the electrical usage of an enterprise, at the same time we lowered the ability of our employees to produce energy in their bodies. Two-thirds of the ATP production needed comes from photosynthesis.

To help people have maximum energy, we need to evaluate the light in our facilities. A couple of options. The best solution is to place a DC incandescent light on everybody's desk. This type of light, DC, is important because it doesn't flicker and no flickering causes less strain. Incandescent lights are critical because they have the full spectrum and they have lower thermal energy. The second option is to place a DC halogen light on everyone's desk; halogen light is full spectrum, but at a higher thermal temperature. People need the right light to perform. So much science is now available, but we need to provide the right light for our teams to shine. I will go into further light details in chapter 9, which focuses on wellness.

Signal about food: What types of food and drinks are you serving?
CM: To get the best possible energy output from your employees, you need to help them consume the best possible nutrition. One-third of ATP production is from nutrition. Getting rid of sugar can have a major effect on a person's energy.

Signal about water: Water is clearly one of the most important factors in terms of what you put into your body, simply because without it you will die within a few short days. Did you know that in terms of the number of molecules, your body actually consists of over 99 percent water molecules! Are you filtering the water? Is your water in plastic bottles? Have you ever looked into structured water and its benefits? Structured water is discussed by Dr. Pollack in his book *The Fourth Phase of Water*.

A simple explanation is the following: Basically, structured water means that *water can form a crystalline structure hundreds of microns thick when associating over certain surfaces, such as the proteins in your cells and tissues.* This means that the more structured water becomes, the more potential it has for enhancing hydration and cell-to-cell communication.

CM: Water fuels the cells and helps power the mitochondria to receive the nutrition they need to power the body. The better the water, the better the energy. Providing a structured water filter in place can have big effects at a cellular energy level.

Signal about nutrients: Vitamin D isn't just a vitamin. It's actually a neuroregulatory steroidal hormone that influences nearly 3,000 different genes in your body. Did you realize that 85 percent of Americans are Vitamin D-deficient?

CM: This deficiency leads to many issues and many lost work hours. Have all your employees download the Vitamin D minder app and have your employees go for 10-minute Vitamin D walks! This is a very simple solution to a big problem. It is back to the light equation: Sunlight + proper workplace lighting can = large effects on the Energy Wellness Equations.

Signal about electricity: Electro-magnetic Fields = dirty electricity = poor health.

CM: I studied electro-magnetic field theory and was always amazed at the complexity of energy layers in our universe. The realization for me that EMF is such a huge problem in our lives has been an awakening over the last couple of years. The electrical devices we are around—computer screens, building systems, lighting, mobile devices, and so on—are affecting us in ways we don't even realize. We can clean up some of this exposure in our workplaces and we all need to dive in and mitigate these unseen risks.

Time, patience, effort, and determination are needed to play the long game of developing the energy economy in your enterprise.

Let's dive into the Energy Drivers.

Energy of Presence

The *Energy of Presence* is vital because listening to signals of your enterprise emanates from being present. Presence today is incredibly challenging. The dynamics of crowd mentality is influencing our behavior more and more. Science and marketing are constantly attacking our ability to process information with desire modification techniques. All this manipulation keeps us always spinning towards dissatisfaction.

Organizations, managers, and employees tend to fixate on always wanting more. No matter how fast our companies are growing, we want more. This constant desire to want things different or better than they are drives tremendous complexity and makes it very difficult for us to be "present" anywhere. We need to be selfless and present to give employees the ability to do something amazing; we need to create positive potential energy and empower people to let the simple truths surface.

My own signal for Energy of Presence is:

Signal: Lost in my Box of Limitations, my BVIs around the desire for acceptance and inclusion left me present nowhere and our corporate systems were gravitating towards disorder.

CM: I used to feel important because I was busy. I was using my energy being busy and therefore wasn't "present" in the organization in a way that drove questioning that would help us function more effectively. Human systems need constant care just like any other system. The second law of thermodynamics has profound implications when applied to managing businesses because it clearly implies that unless effort (i.e., energy) is applied on the various aspects of the corporate activities, there is a high degree of certainty that processes will fail to deliver.

Unfortunately, managers who tend to think in black-and-white terms believe that once a system is in place, it should work without their care. System dynamics are never stable; there is never a time when a system is perfectly balanced. The more energy something takes in your organization, the more entropy it will cause. At some point, total energy needs will overtake total potential energy and a company will fall into disorder and fail.

Albert Einstein is often quoted as saying, "If I had 20 days to solve a problem, I would take 19 days to define it."

As leaders, we need to be present to help free the desire to explore and discover new perceptions in all situations. Asking the right questions frames the entire conversation as an inquiry in which stakeholders are coming together to uncover the best solution.

Fortunately, managers who are good coaches can create teams and human systems around environmental, organizational, and job factors that influence the behavior and desire to explore new things and create a systematic process. People can learn to identify typical problems and correct them without management intervention. To the degree that the manager teaches and coaches employees about these skills, the manager can spend his or her time doing higher-level work. You must, however, be wary of assuming that the system is perfectly balanced and running on its own. This can be a big mistake.

Personal and organizational energy is a truly renewable resource, provided you know how to foster it. Presence positive energy is created moment by moment through our thoughts, feelings, words and actions. A company that is optimistic, collaborative, and prepared for any challenge can drive the positive energy required, but it takes leadership, vision, and hard work to accomplish it.

Signals Around Non-Physical Energy Drivers

Key cultural signals of an enterprise that will function effectively with minimum of energy spent on BVIs:

- **Security:** An honest, trustworthy and authentic environment
- **Autonomy:** Give people the ability to make decisions
- **Cooperation:** Open communication with balanced interchange and mutual understanding
- **Diversity of thought:** Question assumptions to get a variety of perspectives
- **Resilience:** Develop an emotionally resilient environment
- **Feedback:** No judgement

Misuse of energy leads to confrontation between people. In a corporation, this manifests in silos with individuals behaving in self-centered ways to protect their worlds. In business, life, and leadership, our Boxes of Limitations can drive us to complicate things because we are avoiding the truth. By complicating things, we can ignore the data, facts, and knowledge and stay in the BVIs of our Boxes of Limitations.

How do you look at *failures*?
- Unless the failure is catastrophic, most failures can be overcome.
- Forgive yourself, your team, and whoever is responsible and move on. Forgiveness provides the largest release of positive energy into

yourself, your teams, and your business. You stop disorder from continuing with forgiveness and have all your energy focused on creative/growing endeavors

> *I have not failed, I've just found 10,000 ways that won't work."*
> *Thomas Edison*

How does *anger* surface in your organization?
- Consequences of anger
- Closes off communication
- Clouds judgment
- Actions we regret

How is the *fun* part of your culture?
- Are you having fun at your workplace?
- What would make work more fun?
- It needs to be acceptable for employees to have fun at work.
- Are your teams happy even when they are dealing with difficult issues?
- Are people upbeat even when they put their opposing views on the table?

Bad energy organizations tend to be suppressive, unpredictable, and unproductive. Where negative appears, fear prevails. Poor results follow.

- **Leading with Energy**
  Good examples: Positive attitudes, giving credit to others
- **Building Personal Energy**
  Your mental and emotional states are systems that work according to the laws of thermodynamics. When your mind and emotions are using up excessive energy, the system will need more energy to

maintain itself and there will be less energy available for you to be engaged and productive.

- **Limiting Contact with Bad Energy**

  I do this in order to keep my own energy level high. And, when I'm feeling a bit down, tired, stressed, or distracted, I know that I'm all the more vulnerable to absorbing their bad energy. They're unwittingly but effectively leaving a negative mark on our company's culture. You need to help them to alter their energy to the positive end of the spectrum, or help them find another place to work.

> Imagine a company with a growing opportunity in the marketplace and with the unique capabilities to exploit it but whose co-founders are at one another's throats. There's mistrust and a lack of respect that affect the interaction of sales, marketing, finance, and technology and how these teams plan, communicate, and work together. This is an entropy problem. It costs too much energy to maintain the system against this onslaught and the company won't be able to marshal its resources effectively to capture the opportunity. Unless the current energy drains can be freed up, the company will succumb to entropy and perish (specifically, the company loses its ability to integrate—i.e., make sales, meet customer needs, and adapt to changing conditions in the market because the internal friction is too high).

The Manager's Energy Equation

The better my energy is, the better my co-workers' energy is likely to be. The better their energy is, the more fun I have. Consider the following questions to evaluate the type of energy you are fostering within your company:

- Am I being appreciative of the little things going on around me?
- Am I having fun?
- Am I smiling?
- Am I listening effectively?
- Am I giving out heartfelt compliments?

Signal: Is your employee engagement where you want it to be?
CM: Deepening your understanding of energy helps you create a culture where the process is as enjoyable as the results. People are hooked because they are engaged and no willpower is required to stay on track.

According to a worldwide study conducted in 2014 by Towers Watson, the single highest driver of engagement, is leadership. Sustainable engagement requires strong leaders and managers. In companies where both leaders and managers are perceived by employees as effective, 72 percent of employees are highly engaged. In this same study, 4 out of 10 workers surveyed are highly engaged.

In another study, workers who felt unfairly criticized by a boss or felt they had a boss who didn't listen to their concerns had a 30 percent higher rate of coronary disease than those who felt treated fairly and with care.

In 2014, The Energy Project surveyed 20,000 employees and found that employees are vastly more productive if four core needs are met: Physical, through regular opportunities to recharge at work; emotional, by feeling valued for their contributions; mental, when they have the opportunity to focus on important tasks; and spiritual, by doing more of what they do best and connected to higher purpose.

Demand for our time is exceeding our capacity. Work is depleting, and in many ways dispiriting. "Engaged and Fun" works.

From these and many other surveys, you should see that:
- Employees who feel that their managers care are more engaged
- Positive feedback yields 5x increase in performance
- Being fairly treated is vital
- Working on something real matters

The Enterprise Energy Strategy: Playing the Long-Game for Success of Your People and Your Enterprise

The natural order of energy is the same for the corporation as in the universe. Where things become distinctly different is in nature, things only do things out of instinct. The trees grow because they are programmed to grow. The disorder for a tree comes from the environment around it. Does it get water? Is it attacked by bugs? Does it get cut down? For an organization of humans, instinct has a role, but our BVIs play a much larger role and, as a result, are much more prone to failure. We need to make certain our people and organizations don't spend energy and lose time in routine impulsive actions so we are able to develop an organization that has a disciplined approach to protecting our most precious resource: energy.

Now that you're familiar with thinking about energy more broadly you will be able to listen for signals around energy and develop strategies on how to better optimize your corporate energy strategy. The basic Laws of Thermodynamics provide a great platform for driving an energy understanding. If you imagine your enterprise has 100 people, and 60 of those people are required to enable the company to operate, that leaves 40 people available to perform work associated with growing the company. The more people it takes to operate, due to entropy and disorder, the less ability to invest energy in new activities. Keeping an eye on understanding your energy signals will help you optimize your enterprise.

Keep in mind that when an organization has a large amount of internal entropy but temporarily gets more energy through sales, raising capital, or acquiring another company, the company's underlying problems are usually compounded. If you've ever been involved in a bad merger or acquisition, you'll know what I mean. Trying to bypass internal entropy needs is like trying to cure an illness by masking the symptoms with medication. Yes, it can feel better, but if the underlying condition persists, you've got a bigger lingering problem destroying the system from within.

For example, when you're tired (entropy) at work, you may get a cup of coffee. This is a temporary stimulant to get you through the day. However, if you keep going for coffee again and again, your internal entropy needs are simply being masked, not solved, and the stimulating effects of the coffee become less and less. Ultimately, the coffee's acidity eats away at your stomach, affecting your health. Then your doctor recommends you quit drinking coffee, take up drinking herbal tea, and get more rest and exercise to better manage your stress. Similarly, if you can solve the underlying conditions that are causing entropy to increase in your business, you'll roll more energy to the bottom line and have a stronger, more resilient, and high-performing organization.

We each have a finite amount of time and energy to perform integration within our lives, to understand ourselves and others, and to experience the fullness that life has to offer. Awareness of energy allows us to focus on the key areas that drive positive energy and order in our corporations and our lives.

It is about creating systems that function efficiently and maximize output with minimal energy expended. Creating a Wellness Energy Equation for your Workplace,

Key Takeaways

How are you stimulating the energy in your company?

○ Look at the three energy drivers: Physical, Presence, Non-Physical

- What are the natural patterns of each employee and are you designing a program to maximize each person's pattern?

- Are your managers being present?

- Thermodynamics of the workplace is vital to understand

- Net energy is always the same

- Closed systems suffer entropy to become less and less efficient.

- Balancing the total energy economy of an enterprise requires developing new perspectives.

CHAPTER 6

Onboarding Success in the Energy Economy of the Enterprise

Optimizing your onboarding process to drive the most amount of new potential energy and the least amount of Entropy into your enterprise is vital.

The Boxes of Limitations around onboarding include:

○   Driving productivity
○   Caring at all levels in the organization
○   Freedom

In the area of Productivity, we are driving for two main things:

○   Personal productivity: How to get each new hire "in the zone" quickly.
○   Team Productivity: Clear set of guidelines for making decisions.

Signal: Do you just throw someone into the mix and let him or her figure it out?

As enticing as this tactic may seem, it doesn't equal positive potential energy. Early on in our company's development, a new employee started and the manager didn't know he was starting. There was no computer ready and it was a mess. Not only did the new employee not add any potential new positive energy, we had several people scrambling to help him, which caused lost hours of productivity.

CM: When bringing on new team members, you are adding in new potential energy to the system. This new ability can propel things forward. It is new capacity to perform better or do additional work.

The best way to ensure the energy is added in quickly is to have your work processes defined. Each team will have different flows, but each of the teams is centered on eight central themes:

- Optimizing communication patterns.
- Tolerance is crucial. Tolerance equals the will to find out. No biases.
- Unity of Direction. You can't have diversions away from the team's goals and objectives.
- A set of guidelines for making decisions.
- Weekly manager check-ins to drive clear accountability.
- A lightweight roadmap to drive unity of direction.
- Goal setting strategy around the OKR (Objective and Key Results) process.
- Understand the intentions of every person coming into the organization. What I mean by this is that I want everyone to want to be "here." If they are coming to work out of obligation it lacks authenticity. Employees will feel obligated versus empowered, subject to suggestion versus questioning and caring about the truth.

We don't want to rule over employees. We want to provide the direction and let people have the freedom of thinking

Signal: Executives don't want to invest the time and resources into onboarding and ramping new hires.

The most common signal I hear about from corporate leaders is how do they get their executives to want to invest in onboarding?

CM: To minimize wasted resources and energy, investing early in new hires is a very smart investment.

- For me, the answer was really clear. It was rooted in the previously highlighted information. When I was looking at our ramp equation, saying we were going to grow 40 percent or more per year and estimated the number of new hires we were going to have to make, it all boiled down to an energy equation. If we were going to spend a large amount of our company's energy finding great people to join us, then we needed to develop a strategy to enable these people into contributing positive energy as fast as possible.

- Get your teams to be grounded in service of others. When we hire people, they are coming into our culture and it is a privilege to have them join us.

- A few of the realities of new hire success:
  - ▸ Seventy percent of budgets are spent on people.
  - ▸ U.S. employers spend $5.5 billion annually on onboarding processes.
  - ▸ Four percent of new hires don't return after day one.
  - ▸ Sixteen percent of new employees leave in one to three weeks.
  - ▸ Thirty-one percent of new hires leave within six months
  - ▸ Thirty-five percent of companies spend $0 on onboarding

▸ At an average cost to hire of $11,000 for every new employer, the energy drain and financial drain of not having a successful process to get people contributing is very high.3

On the flip side, the data for companies with smart onboarding procedures is compelling:

- 51 percent greater employee productivity
- 50 percent higher retention
- 69 percent greater likelihood employees will be staying three years or longer.

Another CM: All Things Go from Order to Disorder

I worked at a company where we scaled quickly but didn't invest in the onboarding process. Things quickly went to disorder. New employees didn't have clear goals so a great deal of energy was spent trying to figure out what to focus on but very little energy was actually spent on moving the enterprise forward.

The onboarding experience is all about coming together. Coming together starts with trust; we live in a low trust society and we need high trust workplaces. To come together, we must understand the nature of the human experience. Science and technology have changed our comfort and convenience levels, but they can't change our fundamentals of human nature. Humans want a boundary-less opportunity and they want to create meaningful connections. They don't know things the way they are but instead they know them the way they are within them.

Everything is energy; everything you involve yourself in is a result of energy you contribute. How you contribute is as important as what you contribute. You should strive for behaviors that enrich. Behavior is energy and comes in good and bad forms. The behaviors driving the energy out of the team include competition, aggression, and selfishness. Compare these with those that drive energy into the team including cooperation, love and selflessness.

Signal: *We all drive for an ideal.*

We join companies, movements, religions, and so on. What is behind this pursuit of ideals?

CM: What I have come to realize is, at their core, all of our pursuits of ideals are the pursuit of happiness. The new employee is taking this new job; he or she is pursuing more meaningful work, more compensation, a better work/life balance, and so on, but happiness is at the center of all our work decisions. If we can keep in mind that our new employees are in pursuit of happiness, and the corporation is in pursuit of new energy to propel it forward, we can all attain more joy in our lives.

Signal: *The initial interaction with new employees creates an immediate summary of that person.*

The science of the human brain and first impressions gives us the illusion of what we perceive the others to be according to our own Box of Limitations and BVIs. This is rarely the reality of who they are or what they can contribute to our companies.

Social psychologist Amy Cuddy puts it this way, "During our initial interactions...we form a perception of how costly or rewarding a future relationship with the other person would be."

CM: Be aware of this first impression default we all have and keep your mind open.

Some other common signals around Onboarding:

- Employees know what they want from a new hire.
- Everybody knows why the new person was hired and what his or her role will be.
- Employees will figure out the small stuff like facilities, supplies, and so on.
- The immediate supervisor is responsible for the onboarding process.

To maximize the Positive Potential Energy of your new hires, the key goal is integration and orientation.

Define your objectives:
- How long will this process run?
- What experience do you want new employees to feel after day one, week one, month one?
- What do employees need to know about company goals, mission, and values?
- What are the key fundamentals about your business that need to be understood?

Process ideas:
- Create an agenda for your new employee's first week.
- Create a comfortable workplace for your new staff member.
- Provide new employees with a welcome gift.
- Send out helpful information the weeks prior to them starting.
- Help new hires get the lay of the land.
- Block off time for orientation.

- Cover important work processes with the new hire.
- Invest in training. Though the productivity losses can be frustrating, a new hire's first 30 to 90 days on the job should be looked at as an initial training period.
- Allow job shadowing the first few months on the job.
- Conduct your first review and evaluation after an employee's initial 90 days.

Signals that your onboarding process isn't optimized:
- Your stats are below the industry norms for retaining employees.
- Employees aren't contributing as quickly as you had hoped.
- Employees don't know the product, role or responsibilities.
- Employees are not engaged, are missing work, and aren't sharing new ideas.
- There are no internal milestones to measure success
- Staff members have bad attitudes.
- People are consistently failing to hit goals.
- Individuals are not playing well with the team
- People are asking wrong questions.
- Individuals often complain about the job or others.
- People are more concerned about short-term versus long-term success.
- Staff waste time, arrive late/leave early
- Your team is complaining about the new person

A last, and important distinction to make in this is, we aren't trying to create a crowd mentality around joining our enterprises. Crowd science is interesting: you can create passion and action, but you also lose the ability

> *"People don't resist change, they resist being changed."*
> *Peter Senge*

to question. The intelligence of the crowd is actually lower than the individuals within it.

Key Takeaways

- Our goal of integrating people into our organizations is to enable the desire and fire within each new employee to explore and discover the wonders that are open to them pursuing a career within our organization.
- Onboarding people with the least amount of entropy and maximum amount of potential energy is key.
- Creating a process that unleashes Intellectual Suspense and freedom of thought of each new hire.
- The key goal is integration and orientation.
    - How long will this process run?
    - What experience do you want new employees to feel after day one, week one, and so on?
    - What do employees need to know about company goals, mission, values, and so forth?
    - What are the key fundamentals about your business that need to be understood?

CHAPTER 7

Relationships—Engineering Great Performance into Yourself, Your Teams, and Your Environment

Relationships, *"We all got em, we all want them…what do we do with them?"* Jimmy Buffett

Successful Management = Strong Relationships.

Creating an environment, where great performances from yourself, your teams, and your environment all can thrive and grow, starts with understanding some of the bigger signals at play in our society. Information hasn't been set up to operate on truths; it has been set-up to manipulate and control.

Two of the biggest signals we are exposed to are the signals of Propaganda and the signal of Desire Modification. Because of these two signals, today we aren't focusing on the facts. Look at the political arena, advertising, and corporations. So much of the communication is focused on propaganda and desire modification, that we all have a hard time knowing what is real and what is an illusion.

These underlying forces make it all the more important that we strive for our work relationships to be centered on knowing where information comes from and what is being assumed. We must help the people within our organizations regain their desire for Intellectual Suspense by pursing internal truths free from prejudice, free from desires, and free from self-consciousness.

The environmental signal of Propaganda and how PR and advertising use this is a fascinating science.

The **CM** for me was this: The stated objective of Propaganda in the book from Edward Bernays's *Propaganda* is, "the conscious and intelligent manipulation of the organized habits and opinions of the masses is an important element in the democratic society." To truly build an environment where we engineer great performances, we have to make sure we aren't controlling from a propaganda manipulation viewpoint.

On the environmental signal of Desire Modification, when you realize that the science being applied to how to manipulate our desires is rampant in everything in society, you realize there are infinite ways to abuse and brainwash us all and not protect our desire from being modified against our will.

Signal: The desire of that which we don't have is at the root of all suffering.

CM: Realizing the pressure everybody is under from all the forms of desire modification coming at them is vital. Striving to make your workplace a place that people can have trusted relationships based on real information without manipulation is paramount.

The signal of energy in our relationships is another important signal. Energy and the thermodynamic viewpoint leads you on an interesting path of insights. From a global perspective, our global demand economy is having a tremendous impact on our relationship with nature. The entropy happening in nature due to our global demands on resources is having a greater and greater impact.

One example: 60,000 containers ships are sailing the oceans at all times. The noise generated by the engines and ships is causing big effects on animals that communicate with sound. This is one small example of a relationship at the global level. In the bigger picture, our survival depends on the health of the ocean and its ecosystem.

Signal: Relationships are at the center of everything.

CM: In the "separation view" of things, we view our actions as separate from the relationships of others, workplaces, and the environment, but this view of separation is far too simplistic. In fact, everything exists in a highly complex, interdependent, and changeable context and relationship.

For example, the relationships between genes in the human body, rather than only their individual functions, are the key to the countless ways that human genes can produce genetic traits and characteristics. We all need to move to a relationship mentality that drives for energy equilibrium versus wrong relationships in our individual and collective economic lives that drive entropy and disorder.

These relationships offer a guidance system for functioning in harmony and energy balance with natural reality and enduring truths. The body, the corporation, and the universe are electrical in nature and thus susceptible to all external energies it encounters.

Thermodynamic energy in relationships drives the following:

- The need for relationships that drive bonds that create positive free energy

- The need to avoid relationships that drive sameness and ambivalence. These lead to suppression of thought
- The need for relationships that drive spontaneity. Thoughts aren't kept still, but are concentrated and moving towards the unity of purpose.

The "right" thermodynamic relationships drive integrity, resilience, and the synergy of ever increasing knowledge and discovery. It is wrong when it does otherwise.

It is possible to choose right relationships and seek the truth and certainty. Many people, corporations and some communities are doing so. The problem, however, is that in most of our modern societies the majority of people are actively urged, even forced, to choose wrong relationships. And once they have chosen, it is thought we must stay with them.

In our corporations, the actions of each employee affect the entire corporation. We have the responsibility and privilege to consider everybody in the organization in relation to conduct and action on behalf of the organization.

Our evolution over the last 100 years has driven a separation from the whole thought process. The focus on monetary gains and comfort + convenience + conformity hasn't equaled the truth.

We are traveling down a path that has led to ruin societies such as the Mayan, Roman and Easter Island civilizations. As our separation thoughts drive self-focused decisions that drive entropy up and complexity up, the entire relationship/energy system becomes unstable.

We need to drive a transition to relationships with nature, partners, co-workers, customers that shift from relationships based on greed and unquestioned growth to a broader view that drives to the truth of the natural laws of the universe

Three major signals in building relationships are a process I call the Three I's of Relationship Building.

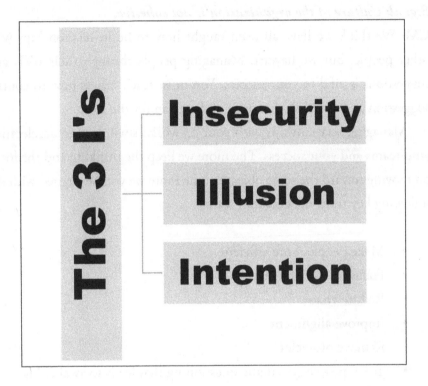

- **Insecurity:** Relationships that were formed out of personal insecurities always create an energy struggle due to the judgement involved—both intrinsic and extrinsic in nature.
- **Illusion:** Relationships that were formed when one or the other person led the other to believe he or she was something he or she isn't. This is a spiral of untruths that always ends poorly.
- **Intention:** Relationships that are based on the truth. These are relationships where all players are able to be truthful, spontaneous, and driving knowledge to new places.

Corporations are about much more than the product or service they offer; they are about people. Learning to work with people is a vital skill.

Signal: Culture of the organization is not cohesive.

CM: We think we have all been taught how to be in relationships with other people, but we haven't. Managing people through their BVIs and suggestions is vital to your success. You must teach others how to control suggestion and establish the unity of direction for the team.

Managing relationships with your co-workers will lead to accelerating your teams and your success. The more we keep the thinking and the focus on moving toward the same objective, the more we will be aligned with the following key traits of successful teams:

- Make people more efficient
- Focus on top priorities
- Reduce chaos
- Improve alignment
- Remove obstacles
- Teach people systematic questioning that leads to awakening decisions
- Invest in the characteristics of the others on your team

CM: The key to it all is teamwork. In all areas of life, teamwork is at the core of it. I wanted my kids to play a team sport to learn the skills but do we ever teach them how to be on a great team? How to lead a team? Relationships drive it all.

A recent MIT study identified the group dynamics, (i.e., relationships) that are present in high performing teams.4 The best predictors of a team's performance are the team's energy, engagement, and exploration outside formal meetings.

Signal: Teams aren't functioning and hitting milestones.

CM: This is fascinating in that it all comes back to thermodynamics. The total energy available is the same. In a team setting, the more energy expended to make the team try to function, the less energy is available to seek out new ideas and input to help the team be successful. This theory sounds pretty basic, but the complexity in the minute-by-minute world of ever-changing priorities is challenging.

Signal: Why do some teams excel over others?

CM: The best way to build a great team is not to select individuals for their smarts or accomplishments but to learn how they communicate so they can shape and guide the team so that it follows successful communication patterns. The ability to leverage a network of relationships leads to success.

Some basic needs we all have that help teams excel:

- To be acknowledged
- To be given feedback
- To be clearly communicated with by others

Some signals that drive dysfunction in relationship dynamics:

- People are much more concerned about potential losses than possible gains. The more complex the decision, the less equipped we are to deal with it.
- People are inclined to stick with their BVIs. They dislike uncertainty. They stick with what they know. If in doubt, they don't do anything. Fear of losses keeps the BVIs in place.
- People sharply discount the future compared to the present. For all but the simplest of decisions, people generally do not

attempt to find the optimal solution, but rather apply simple decision-making strategies and they settle for something that is good enough, rather than searching for the best.

- A key Signal on manager to employee relations: From a large global survey, Edelmans Trust Barometer (http://www.edelman.com/insights/intellectual-property/trust-2013/), we know that 82 percent of people don't trust their boss and 50 percent of employees quit because of their leader. Research has shown that more than 30 percent of leaders act destructively. Such unethical and nonproductive work behaviors are being modeled by our managers. WOW…that means on average eight out of ten of employees don't trust their managers, and yet we expect high performance.

Signals of leadership relationship gaps:
- Lack of integrity. This ripples through your enterprise if your leaders aren't operating with high integrity.
- Excitable and not calm under pressure
- Lack of fairness in treating all employees with the same respect
- No curiosity and being closed to new ideas
- No teaching is happening, leaders are too busy to teach
- Measuring on results only. We have to focus on maximizing the potential.

Finally, engineering great performances requires a need for completely getting rid of judgement. Judgement is the most pervasive relationship destroyer.

We use our judgments about others to make the people we are judging responsible for how we feel. In other words, I would only ever feel better if she changed her behavior instead of me changing my judgment about her behavior. We look at someone else's behavior as a dig against us, instead of something they're doing to themselves.

Signal: Have you ever been to a meeting, and there was one person about whom you felt judgmental?

Maybe it was something he or she did or said, or maybe you had a history with the person? Something caused you to judge the individual. When you felt the judgement kick in, do you want the person to do something different in order for *you* to feel better? Did you want him or her to leave? Or perhaps stay quiet?

CM: Whatever was triggered inside you and caused you to judge them was actually revealing a fear inside yourself. Many of your judgments about people and the world exist because of the lingering emotional issues inside of you. For example, the biggest thing I witness now is people who are in a meeting but not *engaged* in the meeting. They're busy with their mobile phone or computer. Don't judge, just let them do what the need to do and drive to your meeting conclusion.

Signal: Why were so many of my relationships personally and professionally failing?

CM: I had to realize no one wants to be around someone who judges people for being themselves.

Key signals of how judgement shows up in workplace interactions:
- You don't understand the situation and make drive-by decisions
- You set or have unrealistic expectations
- You feel you are superior... separate thinking
- You are closed to new ideas
- You exhibit selfish behavior

Key Takeaways

- Test your relationships against the three Is: Insecurity, Illusions, and Intention
- Are you viewing yourself as separate from your employees or your company? Remember, everything exists in a highly complex and interdependent unity.
- Unity of purpose and direction are vital to building sustainable relationships
- Is judgement part of your thinking? Never depend on others to change who they are or what they do to comply with your standards or who you want them to be. Expecting someone to change for you can and does lead to resentment.
- The core of engineering great relationships is being aware of the macro-environmental signals of propaganda and decision manipulation and the micro-signals around self and team dynamics.
- The relationship dilemma we all face is that—whether with yourself, your teams, or with nature—it all comes down to the more you stay away from judgement, the less entropy you create and the greater freedom your relationships have to be in harmony.

CHAPTER 8
Stop Cheating and Be Satisfied

First, let's look at all the ways we classify the concept of cheating: Bamboozle, Bilk, Burn, Con, Dupe, Fake News, Fraud, Fudge, Hoax, Hose, Hustle, Propaganda, Rip-Off, Scam, Sham, Swindle, Trick, White Wash.... The list goes on and on. When you think of cheating in this broad context you realize it is a massive part of the human condition. That is why being aware of it and addressing it is vital to a great workplace.

Cheating might get you an award, a win, a moment, but it won't get you the truth. Striving to create a "win" for you regardless of principles, ethics or integrity brings casualties.

At their root, the BVIs and the Box of Limitations we draw in each area of our lives and actions are really about cheating ourselves out of Intellectual Suspense and deeper understanding.

The wonderful opportunity as a human being is the opportunity for Choiceability of our actions on our signals. In the world of cheating, you have the Choiceability of a fake reality or of a limitless experience of growth.

A common Signal today is, "Winning is everything; do whatever it takes to win..."

Do you remember Derek Jeter playing in the baseball playoff games in 2010? The ball hit his bat, the umpire gave him first base because he said the ball hit Jeter, Jeter didn't say anything, and took first base. But after the game, he admitted the ball never hit him. I lost all respect for Jeter that day. If he was willing to cheat and violate his integrity on live TV with millions watching him, what was he willing to do if no one was watching?

Sure, he got on base...but he gave up his personal integrity for it. He will never forget it. You know it isn't the truth and you will never forget it. I would have had so much respect for him if he had told the ump, "It didn't hit me; I want to bat." Regardless of the outcome, he would have shown us all that he loved the game more than he loved winning. In society, we still value winning over integrity, but in life, in the long game of loving all things, cheating keeps you from the true freedom of purity of thought. In the Jeter case, he will forever have more complexity in his baseball history because that moment will always be in question. I am sure I am not the only person who lost a measure of respect for him that day.

The BVIs are all rooted in cheating yourself in some way. The spiral towards dissatisfaction drives the need for beliefs and illusions to help us feel better.

Signal: In media, we're being overwhelmed with fake news and fake science. This always reminds me of a quote by Hitler: "Tell a lie loud enough and long enough and the people will believe it."

CM: A common BVI that I grew up with was cannabis is bad and scary. Let's look at the example of cannabis. It was banned in the US by a man named Henry Anslinger. He had a casefile of 200 crimes committed using the substance. The substance got banned, but it turned out his cases were faked. All but two of the cases were proven false and there was no data for the other two cases. So 100 percent of the information used to ban cannabis was wrong; Anslinger knew this and still kept it banned. His cheating, fraud, and bamboozlement have caused many people to be without nutrients and compounds that could have made them healthier and happier.

With the backdrop of cheating and fraud at the government level and at the global power level, how do we operate in our corporations in a way that doesn't follow the example that is being set?

Signal: the signals around cheating start with BVIs around Self-Management. Common signals of cheating ourselves:

- Ever said "I don't deserve it?" Says who? When did you give someone so much power that it's as if he or she planted a voice in your head that says you don't deserve the job, the car, the promotion, or the perfect partner?

- My physical looks need to be different. Stop telling yourself your body doesn't meet the media's version of a perfect body. I recently saw a commercial on Flappy Chin Syndrome. The ad showed us why this was such a bad condition, and then promoted a drug to solve the problem. Until that moment I never even looked at my chin as anything other than a chin! You know what's attractive? Man exists in time, but he must learn to live in the boundlessness. Driving towards a life beyond the limits of BVI's, live in strength, confidence, and caring.

- Ever go to the gym and "work out?" You pretend to be working out, but you don't really push it. In the end, when we waste time, we waste potential. We waste the ability to produce, create, and make a real difference.

- What is your fudge factor? Dan Ariely has conducted some great studies on behavior and exaggerating the facts.5 When you go fishing, do you have a fudge factor? When you go to the gym? When you talk about some accomplishment? When you talk about your kids?

CM: The basic rule we have been told, that "Success Leads to Happiness," is wrong. It is backwards. Happiness leads to success. By cheating, we are faking ourselves into believing that we are successful and hoping it leads to happiness, but it doesn't.

Did you ever cheat in school? You created an illusion that you knew more than you actually did. Remember that feeling you had when you cheated. You can't shake it.

CM: I realized much later in life, that college was more about that you did it, versus what you actually learned. By completing your years of college education, you gained the belief that you were worthy, you were smart, you got accepted someplace amazing so you are above others, and so forth. School had little to do with what I learned and lots to do with simply that I attended college.

Signal: Did you ever cheat in a relationship?

This type of cheating comes in many forms, not just physical cheating, and no matter the form it takes you are still cheating yourself and the other party of the energy in your relationship. Did you violate that trust?

Why is February 13 called Mistress Day? On that day, there is a 271 percent increase in registration by men on the online dating website *Ashley Madison*. On February 15, the website has a 977 percent increase in registration by women!

On February 13, men are stressed and feel they must deliver on February 14. On February 15, women are disappointed by the perceived lack of effort, romance, and affection by their husbands.

CM: In relationships, we often enter into the relationships in pursuit of our expectation of the ideal. When the ideal crumbles in judgement, the relationship dissolves. We see this in the workplace all the time. When you join a new company, you have a high ideal of expectation and then after one month, or six months, the ideal is gone.

Signal: Do you ever cheat at work?

Do you ever cheat on an expense account? Do you ever cheat on the hours you worked?

CM: I have personally done all of these things, and I am not proud that I let illusions control me. The brain seeks out illusions to stop the dissatisfaction with our current situations. As I have seen this play out in my own life and the lives of employees, the eventual cascade of these lies and transgressions catches up to everyone. The energy we burn to keep things in order eventually overwhelms us.

Signal: Thermodynamics re-enters the discussion here; everything is energy in the universe.

Energy can't be created or destroyed, only converted to one form or another. In the world of fake realities and cheating, entropy is increasing in the systems where false information is happening; Cheating energy is the opposite of love energy and creates entropy. The second law of thermodynamics, entropy shows that as entropy production increases, a systems behavior becomes more and more irreversible.

CM: The swirl of cheating and then the actions to either hide the truth or run from the truth cause more and more energy to be expended to keep the façade of the Illusion in place. The swirl depletes you of your opportunity to experience your work, your life in the way in which you are supposed to experience it. I no longer cheat myself in any way. I no longer pollute the truth. I am truthful and I use the BVI testing to drive my awareness when I may be getting fooled into an action to fulfill a BVI, rather than fulfilling the deeper wisdom of the situation. The signals are loud and clear when you stop to truly pay attention

Let's look at some statistics:

Studies have shown 30 percent of all college papers have been plagiarized. Sports scandals involving cheating occur almost daily. Studies show that 50 percent of partners cheat in relationships.

Fifteen percent of annual business fraud involves expense account cheating. Five percent of annual revenues for businesses is lost to some type of cheating.

CM: Cheating doesn't just happen out of the blue. I used to look at cheating as isolated instances. However, I now realize that cheating is a steady stream of signals that escalate over time. These signals are internal struggles with ourselves.

In the workplace, I believe cheating emanates from people feeling that, "I work hard and I am entitled to it." The corporation is so focused on what is happening at the top that it forgets what is needed for the people in the organization. People eventually begin pursuing what they believe they are entitled to get.

Signals that cheating is present in the workplace include:
* **Unhappiness:** Dissatisfaction leads to bad behavior. Listen for the signals of dissatisfaction. A common signal is hearing complaints about the workplace or fellow employees. Another is selfishness.

Most people who are highly satisfied with their jobs and whose needs are being met don't want to cheat.

- **Drama:** People who cheat prefer to ride an emotional roller coaster rather than find joy in emotional stability. They get an adrenaline rush from the figurative bumps and bruises that cause strife and turmoil with their partners, as well as their colleagues.
- **Aloneness:** People need to be around others but people who are cheating prefer to be by themselves.
- **Bullying:** This behavior stifles productivity and innovation throughout the organization. Also, the bullies usually target an organization's best employees because those employees are the most threatening to bullies. As a result, enterprises are robbed of their most important asset in today's competitive economic environment—precious human capital.
- **Avoidance:** Do you see people avoiding obvious things that need to get done? In one recent case, our product roadmap kept getting delayed. Our teams were unclear on the vision and, as a result, didn't want to make decisions for fear of making the wrong choices. The constant pressure to improve performance can have the effect of triggering fears of underperforming and of making mistakes. Perfectionist thinking is avoidance.
- **Hiding the Negative:** Elevating the negatives quickly is vital. When employees start to hide the negatives that is a signal of lack of trust.

Today, modern society has been programed to desire easy. Decoupled from the natural world and mislead by the illusions. Some of the motivators for cheating at work are highlighted below:

- The employee believes he or she can get away with it.

- The employee thinks he or she desperately needs the money.
- The employee feels frustrated or dissatisfied about some aspect of the job.
- The employee feels frustrated or dissatisfied about some aspect of his personal life
- The employee feels abused by the employer and wants to get even.
- The employee fails to consider the consequences of being caught.
- The employee thinks, "Everybody else steals, so why not me?"
- The employee thinks, "They're so big; stealing a little bit won't hurt them."
- The employee feels that beating the organization is a challenge and not a solely a matter of economic gain.
- The employee believes a friend at work has been has been treated unfairly.
- Employees tend to imitate their bosses. If their bosses steal or cheat, then they are likely to do it also.

Signal: How do we violate the trust that drives these behaviors?

Often, we drudge up the past; do you remember the decision long ago that you screwed up? We don't set clear goals and direction and, as a result, we then question things late in the process and cause instability in the organization. We don't listen to salespeople when they tell us the forecast is lower than we want. Instead, we try to will it to the higher goal. This forces us to miss the real signals around our business.... This all leads to energy and entropy. The net energy is always the same, and things are always moving from order to disorder. This trust vacuum in your organization is causing disorder to happen.

Look at how this plays out in each role an honest person plays in the following occupations:

Sales – An honest employee will report issues he or she sees with the numbers, even if it means getting a co-worker in trouble or losing a commission.

Legal – A lawyer who exhibits great character will not inflate his or her hours in order to charge clients more. Lawyers must exhibit integrity and honesty in order to be granted and maintain a license to practice.

Design – Designers with integrity will advise clients when the decisions they are making are against best practices instead of just blindly following client instructions.

Law Enforcement –Without integrity, law enforcement officials would make uneducated and unsupported assumptions and unlawfully gather evidence.

Media – An honest writer values his or her work and therefore will never plagiarize or fudge sources.

Signal: So how do we stop cheating ourselves, each other and our workplaces and find the happiness we all desire?
CM: We need to help people understand that integrity of our decisions matter on the big picture of energy and entropy and matter in day to day leadership.

Great leaders model integrity by being honest and doing what is right no matter the circumstances or the outcome. Integrity requires you to make the right choice, even when you may not receive personal gain from the outcome, and to put your own personal agenda aside for the greater good of the organization and the people. Integrity also requires leaders to admit when they are wrong. Modeling that failure is the way people become better employees. Accountability is vital. When something goes wrong, own it and don't hide from it.

- **Work When You're on the Clock**
  - ▶ Work diligently when you're on the clock, don't socialize, surf the internet, make personal phone calls, text, stop for snacking, or do anything that detracts from work time. Saving those activities for break time will show your manager, coworkers, and customers that you work hard when you're on the clock.
  - ▶ The career website Calibrate Coaching recommends honoring your work hours by not stealing time from your employer. Even if you don't actually punch a time card, focusing on your work responsibilities while you're at your desk, work station, or production area will showcase your strong work habits.

- **Follow Company Policies**
  - ▶ Abiding by company policies is a powerful way to demonstrate integrity. Cutting corners and neglecting to follow workplace regulations can lead to mistakes, problems and even dangerous situations. Your willingness to properly record financial transactions, safely use hazardous or toxic materials, follow company protocol for dealing with clients, perform clean-up or set-up procedures, and properly maintain equipment shows others that you're not just looking for the easy way out.
  - ▶ Establishing yourself as a trustworthy worker who submits to company policies shows your manager and coworkers that you'll faithfully carry out your duties.

- **Respect Coworkers and Build Trust**

- ▶ Respecting those with whom you work shows your desire to create a healthy work environment. Polite communication, appropriate interactions, and respect for coworkers' thoughts and ideas demonstrate your ability to look beyond your own interests to pursue team-centered work goals. As you deal with coworkers honestly and respectfully, you establish a level of trust with them.

- ▶ According to Amy Rees Anderson, a contributor to *Forbes* magazine, those who trust you will spread the word of that trust to their associates, and word of your character will spread like wildfire.

- **Exhibit Responsible Behavior**
  - ▶ Integrity in the workplace often stems from moral and ethical behavior. Making sure there's no reason to question your conduct is one of the best ways to prove that you are an honest and dependable employee.
  - ▶ Avoid using company products or equipment for personal use and submit accurate receipts for travel or meal reimbursements. Don't overpromise what you can't provide, and strive to meet deadlines. Work productively and cooperate during company meetings so you don't appear lazy or apathetic, and don't call in sick when you aren't. By exhibiting responsible behavior, you don't give coworkers or clients any opportunity to question your integrity.

When people are happy at work they:

- produce more

- close more sales
- are better leaders
- receive better performance ratings
- make more money
- are more likely to get promoted
- have more job security
- take fewer sick days
- stay at their organization longer
- are less likely to experience burnout

When people are happy, they are more open to new ideas, see more possibilities, and are less likely to engage in the "fight-or-flight" behaviors that usually come about when they're faced with a stressful problem. They see more around themselves because mood affects the visual cortex in our brains. That allows happy people to move in more innovative ways. It's not that those options weren't available to them before; it's just that when their brain was not in a state of positivity, they literally cannot see them.

In fact, managers who praise their staff are able to achieve up to 30 percent more productivity than those who don't.

Following are some sample comments from director-level respondents on a survey (TLNT Leadership Pulse Project):

- "Most energized when… compelling and inspirational vision exists, when resources, goals and organizations are aligned so that optimal results for customers happen."
- "Challenging projects with deadlines really charge up my energy level."
- "I am feeling like I am spinning wheels in getting things done"
- "I am the most energized when I feel that my work is aligned with the strategic direction of my department; and when I see concrete

evidence that my department's vision is aligned with the larger organizational strategy."

CM: Why do we cheat? I had to look at this behavior in myself. I had lost my dreams and was stuck in the present. I realized that I had to listen to my dreams and not limit them because of my own self disbelief.

We all need to realize we scale our dreams down because of people and circumstances. We don't want to be dissatisfied so we scale them down to ensure we can meet our goals. But that is the opposite of what we *should* be doing. Your dreams aren't big enough; you need to set higher goals. Don't play along to avoid dissatisfaction. Instead, play for bigness, an inspiration to overcome and live with integrity.

Dreams are not merely illusions. They are the higher purpose that God wants for you. Dreams in your heart contain your spiritual "DNA," the very blueprint of who you are. They are the goals and visions that fire your heart and saturate your soul with joy at the very thought of them. What you want to do? How you want to do it? What kind of person do you want to become in the process?

God designed all of us with a dream, but we get stuck in the present, in the BVIs of the world around us and we lose our dreams and get frustrated with the present. We drive for success thinking it leads to happiness and instead it leads to dissatisfaction.

CM: We go for short-term success without realizing that we have wasted months, years or decades following the false BVIs and losing our dream. Life is too precious to waste by building on a crumbling foundation. Many people lose their lives, not by dying, but by squandering their time.

I was cheating myself by focusing on a lot of unnecessary stuff. To be successful in my life and in the workplace, I had to stop cheating myself because I was focusing on unnecessary matters. I had to eliminate the nonessential items and instead invest in the things that would outlast me.

Last, in studies about cheating conducted by Dan Ariely, he found the fudge factor declined to near zero if respondents were reminded of the Ten Commandants before they took on a task where they could cheat. It was the Bible or God; it was the influence of being reminded of what is morally correct. I look to wisdom from many of our past icons as guideposts. Find a list of virtues that work for you. Ben Franklin had a great list. Or read the simple list I have included (that I read each day) at the conclusion of this book.

By reading a list of virtues daily, or another list of virtues like the Ten Commandments, you will keep your mind focused on a strong moral compass and be able to avoid the BVIs that lead you to cheating.

When looking at the world at large, we can no longer stay in our Box of Limitations and be cheated by others who have programmed our thinking. We no longer cheat ourselves by not wanting to have the Intellectual Suspense of each signal.

An interesting example of adaptation and invention is to look to nature as our guidepost. The jungle is the most competitive place in the world and extremely dangerous for all the creatures living in it. Cheating isn't possible; all the plants and animals are constantly adapting new illusions for survival. The animals and plants have leaned on invention as the way to differentiate and survive.

In the U.S., we are turning away from invention of thought, believing it is better to cheat and win than be honest and lose. It's important that you stop cheating yourself, stop cheating in your workplace, and stop cheating everything in life. We all have the ability to justify our actions. Each little action, no matter how small, leads to entropy in the systems in which you are involved.

The quest for success leads to more and more action, which lead to more and more disorder. However, when you pursue character and integrity above success, success will happen. Just as the animals in the jungle, do honest work, drive for invention and truthful knowledge. Let character and integrity provide the inspiration for others in your organization and life.

In the end, we cheat ourselves and those who deserve the real thing.

Key Takeaways

- Start with honesty and simplicity in your life and all your dealings will happen.
- We have the unique Choiceability to choose a fake reality and suffer the entropy or choose the truth and effect a temporary slowing down of the entropy.
- Do you have a list of principles or guidelines that help keep you mind on the path of order and truth? Create your list and read it often. See Appendix B for my list.
- Stop and think about the ways you are cheating yourself, such as stretching the truth, poor nutrition, not focusing on your personal relationships, limiting your vision of what you can accomplish, and so on.
- Stop and ask the following of our workplace right now for signals of cheating:
  - What signals are your teams giving off right now that shows cheating is happening?
  - What more do I need to know?

CHAPTER 9

The Workplace Is Changing and Health Is at a Premium

The continued and accelerated changes in the workforce, from the skills of younger workers coming into the workforce to the technologies of AI and other connected devices and tools, are driving us to look at ourselves and our workforces with new and innovative thinking. Leveraging off the previous chapter about cheating, nowhere is the Box of Limitations greater with the level of unrealized cheating and misguided BVIs at a higher level, than in the area of wellness. The disaster in our health caused by the Box of Limitations of Comfort + Convenience + Conformity ≠ Certainty equation is shocking.

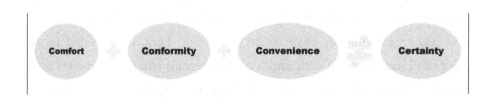

Our society has tried to perfect or monetize what was already perfect in nature. Recreating something that was already perfect is bound to come with consequences. The wellness journey in ourselves and our corporations needs to be about helping people move from a life of disorder, disease and disappointment to a life of order, ease and happiness. The knowledge workers of tomorrow workforce are expected to be amazing at innovation, creativity, Intellectual Suspense and improving the overall business they are involved in.

My CM: If we expect ourselves and our workforces to be amazing at innovation, creativity, Intellectual Suspense, and so forth, we can't simply provide more and more connected devices. Everybody is sicker than ever. We have to dig deeper and drive beyond the power of default action. To drive a culture of health and optimum performance, we need to drive a connection with the energies that will help people attain optimum performance.

My CM: "The more I exercise each day, the more I can eat anything and as much as I want with no consequences." I believed this BVI for 20-plus years until the signals got strong enough. As the company was scaling, I wasn't feeling great. My weight had been steadily climbing three or four pounds per year. My sleep schedule was poor; I was sleeping only four to five hours per night, thinking I just didn't need any more sleep. But in the middle of the afternoon, I felt as if a giant ape had jumped on my shoulders. I could go on and on, but I think you get the picture.

I had to reframe my entire energy equation because I needed more energy and well-being to scale and lead. The signals where everywhere and thankfully, I started to listen to them. I questioned every wellness habit I had and started on an amazing journey both in my personal and work lives. Today, my energy level is off the charts. I'm back to wearing size 34 jeans and I have amazing abs in my mid-fifties! Never thought I would see those again! I work out from seven to fifteen minutes per day, and I'm never tired or hungry. Even better, I haven't gone to a doctor in more than two years. I'm just never sick. I lost 35 pounds, I went from sleeping four to eight hours, my brain has never worked better, *and* I am tireless and healthy. That's a pretty compelling argument to listening to the signals, isn't it?

It comes down to saying, "You Deserve Better" and you can make your life better. To break out of the wellness Box of Limitations, you need to adopt fact-based principles into your everyday life. I do joke about this word, energitarian…but, it is truly what I have become. I focus on every piece of my wellness equation to optimize the energy to excel at life.

Signal: You need to connect how your body functions to how your brain works to how what you are consuming.

It is vital for long-term wellness.

CM: Question assumptions to go from a life of *dis*order, *dis*ease, and *dis*appointment to a life of order, ease, and happiness.

In recognizing what I had to do for myself, I realized I had to develop a workplace where the culture and the environment also embodied health and well-being. Think of this approach like a recipe in cooking. Incredible ingredients create incredible meals. You can create an incredible organization of order, ease, and happiness.

The signals are rampant on the health front in the workplace. Just look around at the increase in diseases. Lost productivity is sky rocketing. Medical payments are escalating.

Common Signals of the Effect of Poor Health at Work

- Is the cost of paid leave escalating?
- Do you have lost productivity due to employees taking time off?

- Are most of your employees in need of a nap in the mid-afternoon?
- Are workplace accidents on the rise?
- Common diseases are ramping up out of control. Since 2000, autism rates have increased; from 1 in 500 to 1 in 68 children are now being diagnosed with autism.
- Employees: 20 percent actively disengaged, 50 percent actively disengaged.
- In 2015, an estimated $550 billion was lost due to poor productivity.
- Forty-five percent of the population—or 140 million people in the U.S. alone—have chronic diseases. That number is expected to increase to 170 million in 15 years.
- The CDC reports that productivity losses linked to absenteeism cost employers' $225.8 billion annually in the United States, or $1,685 per employee.
- Balancing the energy equations can help slow down these issues.

CM: This long list of disease and disorder is amazing. The one that really stood out to me was—Employees: 20 percent actively disengaged, 50 percent actively disengaged.

Are we looking in the wrong place for what is driving the disengagement? It was stated in a book from the 1700s that artificial light was going to create a disengagement from the natural order and it would make us all ill. Is it possible that something so basic as light *can* be at the root of so many of the issues we are facing in today's modern world? I believe it is more the possible.

We have already discussed thermodynamics and entropy but it is also important to learn about balancing the energy in your enterprise and your employees.

The energy drain on employees is significant. If they aren't inputting positive forces from light, water, air, food, they can't combat entropy (Disorder, Disease, and Disappointment). The resulting chaos leads to lost productivity in the enterprise and growing health consequences for the employees.

The signals around wellness could encompass an entire book; I am going to tackle the three biggest signals to look at in the Energy Wellness Equation:

Signal 1: The light in your organization isn't helping people power their bodies in the optimum way.

As we discussed earlier, two-thirds of our cellular ATP production comes from photosynthesis with the exposure to the right kind of light. I am going to breakdown light in detail to help you understand what this is all about:

Light for humans powers everything, from our circadian clock, to our behavioral systems, to our healing responses. New findings from photobiology is forcing us all to update our BVIs of the way our bodies process light. Evolution happened under very strict processes of light and human life is very adapted to distinct photonic set of conditions. We are now all living under the illusion that light is light. We live our lives where 24 hours/day our bodies can see fake light and do not know what is day and what is night. A LED light isn't a full-spectrum bulb; the light from your computers, phones, and tablets are largely blue light dominant and high in thermal temperature.

CM: Cellular energy production can be increased with exposure to 500nm to 850nm light spectrum. Most LEDs are missing this part of the light spectrum and in many office environments we are not getting the light we need to maximize our energy equations.

The story of light today is a fascinating story into Intellectual Suspense. For me, it led me all the way back to my electronic engineering roots. Recasting the body in my mind in terms of a semiconductor and all the signals coming into it impacts its electrical operation was fun and exciting for me. I spent many years working in the semiconductors field and getting my mind wrapped around the body as a biological semiconductor that absorbs and emits light has been the best part of my journey so far.

Most of our light sources in the workplace are blue light dominant. The false light and false heat from the blue lights sends signals to the body that start a chain reaction.

The chain reaction on blue light in nature is, when the sun rises, blue light (UV) is present with red (infrared light). Your body takes the light (Frequency) signals and sets of a series of chemical reactions; blue resets the circadian clock to cycle off melatonin and cycle on cortisol. The presence of blue light and thermal energy from the sun also tells the body that infrared light is present, because with the sun they come together, and our hormones were created to offset the infrared light.

In a false light world, this chain reaction of blue light resetting the circadian clock and triggering hormone release is the root of a lot of our issues with disengagement and illness.

Did you know that our eyes have four million red light receptors, two million green light receptors and one-hundred thousand blue light receptors? Our bodies are designed to take in less blue light, but yet our fake light world is blue light dominant!

CM: Once I started to realize the signal that light was for my bodily operations, light was no longer light. I transformed my nutrition of light to be a regimented, nutritious process focused on maximizing my energy:

My daily routine is now:

- I wake up and turn on DC incandescent light.
- At sunrise, I take 10 minutes looking to the left of the sun to reset my circadian rhythm for my body to tell the melatonin to ramp down and cortisol to ramp up.
- I turn on the DC incandescent light on my desktop at the office.
- I turn down the color temperature on my laptop.
- I enable the blue light blocker on my phone.
- I take trips outside for 10 minutes to maintain my circadian cycles and stimulate vitamin D production.
- After 5 p.m., I limit blue light. Read before sleep to a DC incandescent light.

Since starting this routine, my sleep, energy and positivity around life have transformed.

Let's talk about the most common types of light we are all interacting with LED, sunlight, and incandescent lighting. Understanding what effect each of these has on our biological rhythms is vital. When I started looking back over time, I found articles written in 1975 clearly stating the perils of artificial light. I found research in the late 1800s showing the power of light and color therapy. I found books as far back as the 1700s discussing the dangers of artificial light. But we assume that lower energy usage is king, so we blindly implement artificial light without understanding the biological consequences.

Let's look at how each of these lights affects our natural rhythms.

Sunlight: Thermal 5,600K; Continuous spectrum. 290nm to 1000nm

Incandescent: 300nm to 750nm; temperature of 2850 kelvin. Full-spectrum bulb. Energy usage 5 percent to light, 95 percent to heat. Used with DC power, no flicker and very clean light.

LED: Typically flickers at low freq, causing eyestrain and other issues. A higher thermal reading of 3000+. Blue freq dominated. Since LEDs have virtually no infrared light and have an excess of blue light that's generated, we have a shortage of near-infrared range, which affects health in a number of important ways. For example, it helps prime the cells in your retina for repair and regeneration. Near-infrared light also penetrates the skin and enters the chromophores molecules. Chromophores are found in the mitochondria and in activated water molecules. This is involved in energy production within mitochondria. Adenosine triphosphate (ATP)—cellular energy—is the end product.

So, with lots of blue and little infrared, two-thirds of ATP production needed from light doesn't happen.

CM: Focusing on energy savings will lead you to the wrong lighting solutions to maximize workforce productivity.

We want engaged, creative teams. If we provide artificial lighting, which has been studied for hundreds of years and proven to make people disengaged and ill, we have to focus on the light.

Signal 2: What nutrition are you providing to your employees?

Eighty percent of a person's successful health and weight control is based on the nutrition they take in, not on fitness. One-third of the ATP energy product comes from nutrition.

CM: I had this equation wrong. I used to workout 1.5 hours/day. And ate anything I wanted. But I was always gaining weight. Then, I gave up gluten, sugar, and glyphosate. I lost 35 pounds in 6 weeks and work out 7 minutes/day…and I feel amazing.

The nutrition signal is a complicated and long one. The quality of our food supply is in incredible danger. The multi-prong approach to basic nutritional health in the workplace I recommend is to start with the basics:

- **Water:** Improve the quality of the water you drink. The body is 70 percent water. Drinking tap water, water from plastic bottles, and so on all come with many health hazards. Start by drinking water from a filtered water source. Ultimately driving towards a structured water solution is most desired.
- **Sugar:** Remove the soda machine, remove the sugar snacks.
- **Organic produce:** Remove as much glyphosate out of the food as possible.

Last, many of the Boxes of Limitation assumptions we have all made around nutrition are dead wrong:

- Fat is bad
- Carbs are good
- Pesticides are safe

Signal 3: Fitness
CM: The 1-plus hour working-out strategy wasn't necessary. I now vary my movement routine around many different practices.

A 4- to 7-minute burst workout 4 mornings/week

A 3-nights-per-week yoga stretching routine

A couple of times per week, I do the Foundation Training routine

I am in now better shape and invest significantly less time than at any other point in my life.

To help drive optimum performance and create teams that have high engagement with life and with work, here are six simple strategies to take that will produce immediate gains in your personal and your workplace wellness:

- A few short workout breaks: These will stimulate the brain, the immune system and circulatory systems.
- Healthy foods: Eliminate sugar, gluten, and go for organic produce.
- Using the Vitamin D minder app: This app will train employees to go outside 10 minutes per day and get their Vitamin D to help with cellular energy.
- Take Vitamin C in the right doses: Since I started doing this two years ago, I have not gotten sick once. I used to get sick two or three times a year, losing at least 10 days per year. That means that three percent of my life was spent feeling sick! When I realized I no longer wanted to lose three percent of my days feeling sick, I got out my Box of Limitations and found a simple natural solution that has given me that three percent back! Imagine the productivity gains if all employees no longer get sick!
- Rest: Time off is essential to optimal brain function. I used to work 80-plus hours a week but now I work more like 40 hours. There is no doubt that I have more focus, clarity, and am more efficient. Teach employees how to maximize their work time and make time away from the office a priority.
- Light: There is tons of research available. Follow my routine for a daily dose of the right light equation.

Show people how to start listening to the signals and start to take action. Leading by example drives change. It is slower than you would hope, but everyone needs a way to start challenging their BVIs. Seeing you as an example, gives them the ability to have Intellectual Suspense and the desire to challenge their BVIs.

"Some people are stronger in their ignorance than in the seeking Intellectual Suspense and new perceptions."

Remember, "Conquering others takes force, conquering yourself is true strength." (Lao-Tzu, Chinese philosopher)

The cost of lost productivity because of unhealthy employees may actually be even greater than the additional healthcare costs accrued by these employees. According to an article in the *Harvard Business Review*, "A 2009 study by Dr. Ronald Loeppke and colleagues of absenteeism and presentism among 50,000 workers at 10 employers showed that lost productivity costs are 2.3 times higher than medical and pharmacy costs."

Key Takeaways

- Moving from disorder, disease, and disappointment, to order, ease, and happiness in your energy wellness equation is vital and easy.
- Our BVIs around what drives wellness and maximum energy are so far off-base.
- Using the old views of biological wellness isn't working. We have to use our Choiceability to drive to new understandings.

Of all the things discussed in this book, busting through the Box of Limitations around wellness has been the most impactful on my performance. My old belief of "matter doesn't matter" was so wrong. I now realize that each piece of nutrition I consume has varying levels of stored energy and nutrients for my body. The entire game is to consume matter that is the easiest to process with the highest nutrient content; i.e., the matter that causes the least amount of entropy and stress on my body to drive for maximum energy and longevity.

CONCLUSION

First, I would like to thank you for the time you have invested reading this book. I truly hope the concept of Signals, CMs (Cauliflower Moments), and a Box of Limitation around your BVIs have awakened your desire to break out of the beliefs you have built in your organization and in your life. Desiring the Intellectual Suspense of being open to new perceptions has been the most invigorating process of my life.

As this whole process started unfolding for me, I realized this was much bigger than I am. These concepts and these issues aren't new. As I awakened to questioning my Box of Limitations, I found amazing insight in works from people like Rudolph Steiner, Jacob Boehm, Wilhelm Reich, Manly Hall, and others. All experienced the same issues in their lifetimes. Even in ancient civilizations like the Mayans and Egyptians, there was a battle for the control of the human mind.

In the vein of listening to signals, this book is a manifestation of that process. I spoke at an event and was mobbed at the stage afterwards by people saying I had helped them start to question their enterprise in new ways. I came home and thought, "Wow...maybe I can really help people." I found out that many authors and speakers use a difficult event in their lives to help others get through difficult times in theirs.

I went to school to study Electronic Engineering, I took one English class, and I never expected to be writing a book. I firmly know that these concepts and information contained in this book aren't mine. The knowledge is inherent in the universe in which we all live. I just tuned into it and started listening.

Listening to your signals = being open to new perceptions. "Choiceability" is a word I coined to help me think each time a signal comes into my life: Every individual has to decide the choice between easy and sticking to Comfort, Conformity, and Convenience versus seeking the Intellectual Suspense of not knowing. You have to decide what will rule you in your life and business.

Comfort + Convenience + Conformity ≠ Certainty. As I have explained, we have moved from away from desiring new perceptions. We live in a time in which many people and entities are trying to control us with messaging that can both diminish our growth and take away the truth.

The Latin prefix *dis-* means "to take away." The trio of Disorder, Disease, and Disappointment take our freedoms. Realizing that entities and global powers are using propaganda, desire modification, and other tools to prey on our human design flaws and create BVIs that make sense for them (but not sense for you and your organization), is vital.

The best part of this process is that the Intellectual Suspense and the Choiceability of questioning of your BVIs is free! You need to release yourself from the things that have been taken away from you. Distortion of the facts is the biggest barrier to freedom of thought.

In the workplace, we need to lead our employees and our companies away from Disorder, Disease, and Disappointment. If we expect employees to be highly engaged, imaginative, and satisfied with their work, we can't ignore the outside signals and still expect the best.

To get myself away from the "*dis*" lifestyle, and get back to freedoms, I had to move from managing activities to leading. Leading means growing, coaching, and mentoring. Moving from managing work to leading changed my ways of questioning, and I began to ask what else I needed to know.

Disorder, Disease, and Disappointment have all been driven into us via other people and we are paying a tremendous cost for these BVIs.

I was trapped in my BVIs for more than fifty years; there were many warning signals that I completely ignored. Fortunately, I got rid of just enough of my ego to allow myself to start questioning and accept that it wasn't about me…and that I needed to change.

I originally looked at my missed signals as failures. I failed to keep my weight down, even though I worked out an hour or more every day. I had failed at work because I left a company when I was frustrated and unhappy. I was asked to leave a company because I wasn't acting in ways that aligned with its goals and purpose. My personal life was also filled with many lies and while there were many signals, I just kept thinking I was a failure. My nutrition quality was horrible; I was eating tons of carbs and very little vegetables. I was sleepy all the time, and yet I could only sleep four hours a night. I felt that I was just different.

But all these "failures" were truly not failures of my abilities, or my self-control, or my lack of luck. They weren't "failures" of a bad design in my body. They were limitations I had placed *on myself* from my lack of questioning and trying to stay in my BVIs, from being comfortable and functioning within the operating system I had developed. It was essentially a battle of myself against myself.

Now, I have created a simple rhythm for myself so that on a daily basis, I am ready to question signals coming in and welcome the adventure of the day ahead:

My daily list for allowing signals to drive me to new perceptions is the following. In the morning, I set up my entire day with one simple question:

What is the one thing I will get done today, no matter what?

Instead of multitasking and maintaining a list of way too many things, I highlight the one goal. This easy adjustment has allowed me to get rid of the Disorder and Disappointment that came from my inability to complete everything (on my list) every day.

After I get my one thing established, I read my daily list in Appendix B. When the day begins, I approach each signal with Choiceability in mind. I ask the following questions:

The questions I use for each signal that comes in against a BVI

- Am I open to getting new information about this signal?
- Is this something I know, or think I know?
- Where did my BVIs come from on this topic?
- What more can I or should I know about this?
- What am I supposed to understand here?

To effect sustainable change, we must understand the higher-level issues at work. When you feel your organization or yourself heading towards disorder, you need to realize you are battling the basic laws of thermodynamics that states all systems head toward disorder.

We all believe in the reliability of the sun; even when it isn't shining, we believe it will come back. God put truth in all of us. Have faith, and by faith we persevere.

The key to shedding the "*dis*" in your life is to question where your BVIs have come from. All knowledge comes from another human. This doesn't mean he or she was right or had your best intentions in mind. It just means it was what the individual believed or wanted you to believe.

Truth is the most magical of all properties. When someone has the truth on his or her side, you can't change it. The truth will do the work. Think back to each experience you have had that has been a success. You succeeded because you were true in the situation. Some people think success is about knowledge but gaining knowledge is only as good as the belief you acquired while obtaining that knowledge. This is why you can't take shortcuts in anything that is important to you. We are all here to learn and shortcuts don't allow that learning to guide you to the truth. The magic to an unstoppable life is to seek out deeper truths. The truth will do the work.

Listening to signals and questioning your signals lead you to Cauliflower Moments of new perceptions.

We all have something great to give. Give energy to those around you and help them have order in their lives, and you will have the success you are searching for. Realizing that all matter we consume matters: we need to consume things that provide us with the most amount of energy, with the least amount of entropy to our bodily system. With regard to relationships, realize they are about leading sensual lives together. Sensual means being delighted in the exploration of all our senses and willingness to be in the suspense of the unknown together.

I hope this book helps you find the desire to realize the Box of Limitations you have built in each area of your life. We all love great adventure movies, and I used to as well...but now, I recognize the everyday adventures of opening up to the Intellectual Suspense that each signal brings are the moments you realize what freedom really means and how impactful the Choiceability of questioning your BVIs can be to your life and the lives of many around you. Our technologies and cultures have made things too easy, it is time to question and makes things more difficult.

FIGURES

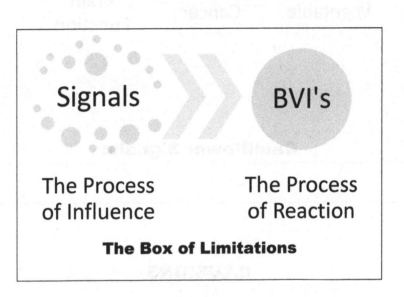

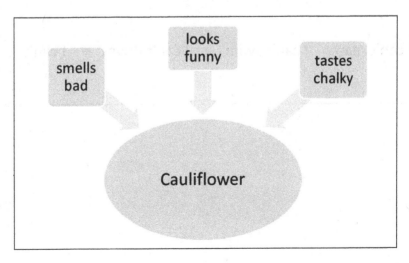

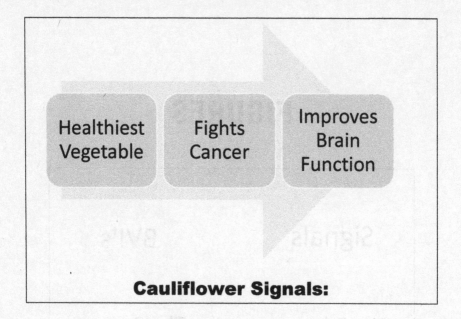

Cauliflower Signals:

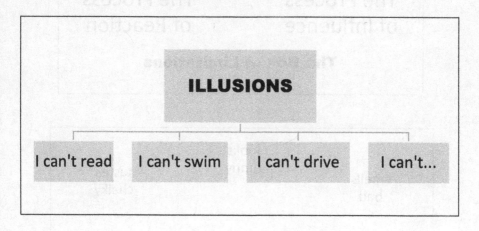

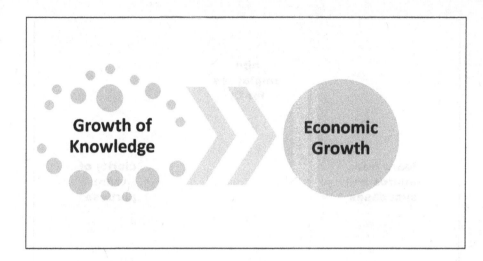

Information	• testing illusions • gathering data
Experiments	• try different ideas • take risks
Experience	• what happened? • why?
Epiphany	• real results • make key decisions

hire employees for fit

clarity of team purpose

learn from failures and successes

build culture and values

freedom of intellectual curiosity

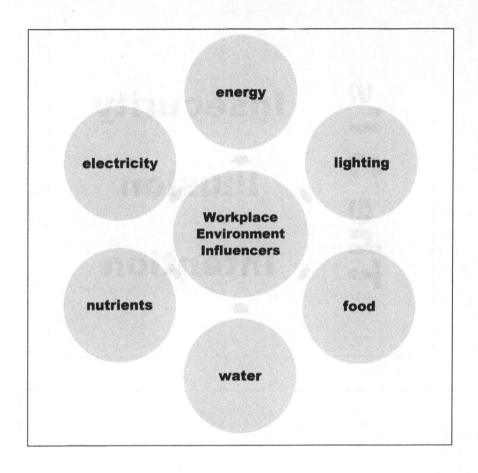

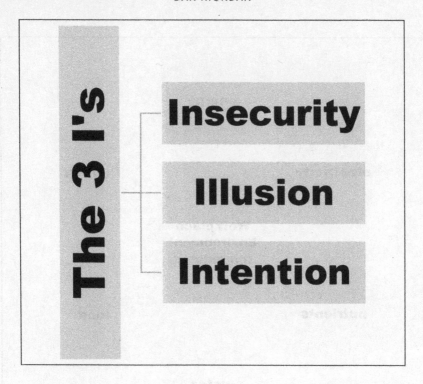

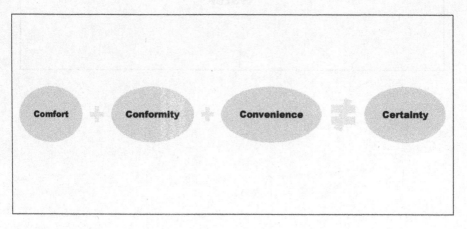

APPENDIX A

Questions We Ask on Weekly Check-Ins

Simple ratings for the following:

- Overall Weekly Performance: Needs Improvement, Meets Expectations, Exceeds Expectations
- Highlight Biggest Accomplishment for the Week
- Highlight Areas for Improvement
- Other Comments: Free-Form Input Area

APPENDIX B

My Daily List

- Drive for Intellectual Suspense
- Enjoy freedom from certainties
- Control impulses: moderation in all things
- Order in all things: thoughts, actions, truth
- Be free of all judgement
- Optimize Energy in my life: nutrition, eating, air, sleep, truth
- Stop and appreciate a nature moment each day: sunrise, birds flying. Wonder is all around us.
- Love all things

APPENDIX C

Questions to Ask
at the End of Each Day

- Have I been my best today?
- Did I thrive in Intellectual Suspense today?
- Did I serve others today?
- Did I judge anything today?
- Did I improve my Character today?

END NOTES

1. Selena Larson, The Daily Dot, Jan, 2016: theweek.com/articles/597663/
   how-facebooks-memory-affect-emotional-wellbeing
2. Whats new with Small Business, 2016 SBA Data:
   https://www.sba.gov/sites/default/files/
   Whats_New_With_Small_Business_Text_Version.
3. February 2014 survey by BambooHR
4. Alex "Sandy" Pentland, From the April 2012 issue, The new science of
   building great teams.
5. Dan Ariely author of the books Predictably Irrational: The Hidden
   Forces That Shape Our Decisions, The Upside of Irrationality: The
   Unexpected Benefits of Defying Logic at Work and at Home and The
   Honest Truth About Dishonesty: How We Lie to Everyone – Especially
   Ourselves.

ABOUT THE AUTHOR

Dan Riordan is currently COO of ThinkHR, a company that develops HR knowledge solutions. Prior to taking that position, Riordan held operational leadership positions for 25-plus years at companies including Level 5 Networks, Skystream Networks, C-Cube Microsystems, and Sierra Semi-conductor.